BEIJING

Cityscopes are concise, illustrated guides that provide an overview of a city's past as well as a focused eye on its present. Written by authors with unique and intimate knowledge of the cities, each book features a chronological history to the present day. Also including a section of essays on key places or aspects of the city today – from museums to music, public transport to parks, food to fashion – the books offer fascinating vignettes on the quintessential and the quirky, as well as listings of key sites and venues with the authors' own commentaries. Illustrated throughout with contemporary photos and compelling historical images, Cityscopes are essential companions to cities worldwide.

Titles in the series:

Beijing Linda Jaivin

Buenos Aires Jason Wilson

cityscopes

Linda Jaivin

BEIJING

REAKTION BOOKS

Published by Reaktion Books Ltd
33 Great Sutton Street
London EC1V 0DX, UK

www.reaktionbooks.co.uk

First published 2014
Copyright © Linda Jaivin 2014

The writing and production of this book was greatly assisted by Australian
National University professor Geremie R. Barmé and his Australian Research
Council Federation Fellowship 'Beijing: China's Heritage and the City
as Spectacle'

Printed and bound in Hong Kong

A catalogue record for this book is available from the British Library
ISBN 978 1 78023 261 4

OPENING IMAGES: pp. 6–7: the Forbidden City moat in snow; p. 8 top: *hutong* tour by the lakes at Shichahai;
p. 8 bottom: Tiananmen Square during the National Day Holiday; p. 9 top: changing of the guards, including plain-clothes
police, at Tiananmen; p. 9 bottom: backstage at the Peking Opera; pp. 10–11: Tiananmen Square, view from Tiananmen Gate.
At the right is the Great Hall of the People, in the right foreground is the winged column known as a *huabiao*, in the centre
background the Monument to the People's Heroes and, behind that, the Mao Mausoleum; p. 12: the CCTV Headquarters;
p. 13: Chinese New Year temple fair lanterns, early 2014, the Year of the Horse; pp. 14–15: artist Xu Bing's *Phoenix*,
built from materials collected from construction sites in Beijing between 2008 and 2010; pp. 16–17: the Forbidden City.

CONTENTS

The Back Lake at Shichahai.

Prologue

Peking is a jewel city, a jewel city such as the eyes of man have not seen before. It is a jewel city of golden and purple and royal blue roofs, of palaces and pavilions and lakes and parks and princes' gardens. It is a jewel set with the purple sides of Western Hills and the blue girdle of the Jade Fountain stream and centuries-old cedars . . . In the city are nine parks and three imperial lakes, known as the 'Three Seas', now thrown open to the public. And Peking has such a blue sky and such a beautiful moon, such rainy Summers, such cool, crisp Autumns, and such dry, clear Winters! . . . It has colour – colour of the old and colour of the new. It has the colour of imperial grandeur, of historic age and of Mongolian plains . . . It has miles upon miles of city walls, forty or fifty feet broad at the gates. It has gate towers and drum towers, which announce the evenings for the residents. It has temples, old gardens, and pagodas, where every stone and every tree and every bridge have a history and a legend.

The great bilingual writer Lin Yutang wrote that in the 1930s, in his essay 'Captive Peking'. Today, the jewel sparkles less brightly. On the city's many bad air days, the pollution is so thick it can blur the edges of the buildings across the street, never mind the Western Hills. Beijing's imperial grandeur can be equally hard to summon. Its denuded palaces and temples and other historic monuments are dwarfed by high-rise developments that have nothing to say about its historic age and which have swept outwards over the Mongolian plains like a tide of cement, tile and glass. Its famous walls have given way to subway tracks and highways, its legendary gate towers are mostly remembered in the names of train stations. Evening is announced not by bells and drums but the glow of neon and the tightening gridlock of the city's infernal traffic.

And yet every so often, a beautiful blue breaks out in the sky like a miracle and the palace roofs and lakes sparkle, or fresh snow falls, and everything looks clean and magical. Within the remaining courtyard gardens, peach and crab apple trees still bloom in spring and the branches of the pomegranate and persimmon trees hang heavy with fruit in the autumn. You can still buy roast chestnuts and sweet potatoes from street pedlars as the days grow cold and short, and sour plum juice on long summer days to keep the heat at bay.

In Beijing, if you know what you are looking and listening for, you can read history in private doorways and hear its echoes in public parks. Drink coffee at Ritan Park and you walk where the emperor once performed rituals at the Altar to the Sun; wander the aisles at Walmart in Caishikou and you are crossing the old execution ground. The most careless urban development – and urban development has rarely been more careless than in Beijing – can't obliterate the legacy of the city's 3,000 years of history, or the five dynasties that made Beijing their capital. And so this tough, beleaguered city continues to enrapture and enthral those for whom its richer, bigger, more seductive rival Shanghai appears but a glamorous parvenu.

The people of Beijing have seen it all – cycles of prosperity and decay, wise rule and corruption, order and chaos. They've been treated to the greatest of grand spectacles, from imperial processions to Red Guard rallies and Communist Party congresses. Proximity to power has brought some citizens wealth and others grief, some wealth and then grief. Its history is soaked in blood as well as glory.

Nomads – Mongols, Manchus and others – frequently raided Beijing from the Great Walls meant to keep them out. For centuries they ruled it as well, bequeathing to Beijing a hybrid culture and an archetypal personality that is perhaps rougher-and-readier than that of many other parts of China, yet which is also urbane, dignified, big-hearted, witty and playful.

The intoxicating Beijing dialect reflects this in its inborn courtesies, its unique burr, its wit and pace. The language of Beijing, to quote the writer Liu Yong, 'always seems spoken in the carefree, leisurely manner of one who is enjoying a cup of green tea in the warm sunshine of a late autumn afternoon'. (On the subject of language, 'Beijing' is what became of 'Peking' after 1979 when the Communists made *pinyin* the standard romanization system for the spelling of Chinese names.)

Beijing shares a latitude (39°54′N) with Philadelphia in the U.S. and Toledo in Spain. It's a northern city with northern habits. Its people have a taste for mutton, yoghurt and wheat (steamed and fried breads, noodles and dumplings) as well as fierce grain spirits, all of which come together in the typical winter meal of mutton hotpot accompanied by sesame buns and shots of potent *erguotou*.

Beijing's four seasons are distinct and in harmony with the divisions of the Chinese lunar calendar. Neglect the advice of the traditional almanac to switch to winter hats on a particular day and you'll have cold ears. Winter nights may well dip below –10°C and summers can be stifling, with the mercury climbing into the high 30s. Spring brings not just rain but epic sandstorms, and autumn delivers just the sort of delicious, green-tea weather described by Liu Yong.

Beijing has been the home, native or adopted, of many of China's most famous and influential artists, thinkers and writers, including Cao Xueqin, whose *Dream of the Red Chamber* is widely acknowledged to be the greatest novel in the Chinese language; the early twentieth-century literary giant Lu Xun; and even the 2010 Nobel Peace Laureate, the imprisoned dissident Liu Xiaobo. It's been both the citadel of state power and the crucible of iconoclasm in China.

China has no time zones: Beijing time is China time. Beijing has often represented China both to itself and to the world. During the Republican period, 1912–49, China's emblem was the imperial Temple of Heaven; today it is the

Gate of Heavenly Peace (Tiananmen) and the Great Wall.
Even its tragedies are emblematic. The burning by French
and English troops in 1860 of the imperial garden palace,
the Yuanmingyuan, remains the single most searing symbol
of a century and a half of humiliation and exploitation by
Western (and later Japanese) imperial powers in the Chinese
national imagination. Marco Polo's awestruck descriptions
of 'Cambulac' (Beijing), photos of Nixon on the Great Wall,
the Tiananmen protests of 1989 and the opening ceremony
of the 2008 Olympics have all helped to shape the image of
China to the world outside its borders. Although the great
diversity of China could not possibly be contained in any
one city or village, Beijing's story is in many ways that of
China itself.

Winter in the *hutong* near the lakes of Shichahai.

Nanluoguxiang in winter.

1 Wild Years

I n the lower basement of the Malls at Oriental Plaza in Beijing's bustling shopping centre of Wangfujing, beneath the designer shops and below the Wonderful Food Court, sits a pocket-sized museum. At its centre is a fenced-off square of packed earth. Cooking fires lit 24,000 years ago have left scorch marks on the ground; discarded animal bones lie alongside abandoned stone tools. In the first years of the new millennium, workers excavating the plaza's foundations discovered the Stone Age site. After archaeologists surveyed the rare finds, the mall's developers agreed to preserve a tiny part of what became a sub-stantial dig. The Wangfujing Palaeolithic Museum is a reminder that people have been coming to this area to hunt and gather from the Stone Age through to the Plastic Age.

At the time those cooking fires were lit, the Yellow River flowed closer to the place we call Beijing than it does today. That patch of ancient dust was once part of a fertile alluvial plain roamed by wild pigs, buffalo, sheep and deer. The rivers and streams teemed with fish, turtles and beavers. Grass, wildflowers and trees laden with nuts and fruit scented the bright, clear air. This was the world of the early humans descended from the hominids known as Peking Man, *Sinanthropus pekinensis,* who may have been around as long as 780,000 years ago.

Peking Man rewrote evolutionary history in the 1920s when a Swedish geologist discovered hominid teeth at Zhoukoudian's Dragon Bone Mountain in Fangshan county, 42 km southwest of the capital. Chinese and foreign archaeologists soon found more teeth as well as bones, skulls, skull fragments and tools. As they put the pieces of the puzzle together, the scientists

Hunting and gathering the old way: a mural in the Wangfujing Paleolithic Museum.

discovered that these hominids had a similar skeletal structure to our own and a bigger brain than either Java Man or South Africa's *Homo habilis.* They lived in communal caves in the mountains for protection from the sabre-toothed cats, wolves, panthers and bears that also thrived in this rich environment, venturing occasionally on to the plains to hunt.

Scientists were still excavating at Zhoukoudian in 1937 when the Japanese invaded from the north, crossing the nearby Marco Polo Bridge. Forced to abandon the dig, the team, led by the Jewish German-American anthropologist Franz Weidenreich, retreated to a lab at the Peking Union Medical College to study their finds. By then they had collected tens of thousands of tools as well as skull and bone fragments from almost 40 individuals of both sexes, including adolescents and one who had lived past fifty. In 1941, with the United States poised to enter the Second World War, Weidenreich needed to return to America. He instructed his colleagues to make replicas of all of the fragments and send them to him in the U.S. The remains themselves were to be crated for shipment out of Japanese-occupied Beijing.

In the confusion of wartime, Peking Man went AWOL. Was the disappearance the result of bumbling on the part of the U.S. Marines to whom the crates were entrusted? Did conniving Japanese scientists steal the relics? Were they buried under a garage at the American Embassy? Hidden in the Taklamakan Desert, as posited in Nicole Mones's novel *Lost in Translation*? Secretly sold to an American collector? Do they sit, as one rumour has it, on the mantelpiece of an elderly Chinese revolutionary? All that remains are the replicas, the theories, and enough mystery to fuel the mad fires of creationists who claim that the fact that no one can produce the actual relics is proof that the whole business, and the theory of evolution itself, is a hoax. If any reader knows the truth, please contact the Fangshan county government, which is offering a reward for the return of its natives.

Later excavations at Zhoukoudian (now a UNESCO World Heritage site) turned up evidence of an even older hominid, nicknamed 'Mountaintop Caveman', and other, post-Peking Man hominids as well. For the record, none bear the slightest resemblance to the oversized gorilla with a soft spot for a

Entrance to the Peking Man Museum at Zhoukoudian.

leopard-swinging blonde that stars in the cultish Hong Kong film *The Mighty Peking Man* (1977). They had more in common with the blonde: they too wore animal skins and jewellery fashioned from bones and shells. By the Neolithic age these early humans began settling on the plains, where they cultivated grain (probably millet – a staple of Beijing home cooking to this day), domesticated animals and coaxed clay into pottery.

Chinese history formally kicks off around 2700 BCE with the appearance of the quasi-mythical Yellow Emperor. This legendary 'great ancestor' of the Chinese people waged fierce battles against his rivals (who included horned demons and giants) to become the first ruler of a dominion not yet called China. These supernatural battles, in which floods and drought were part of the combatants' arsenal, may have been fought on the site of today's Beijing. As the accounts were recorded several millennia later, we can't know for sure.

Historical ground firms under the Shang dynasty, which began around 1600 BCE. The Shang claimed a subordinate state called Yan (meaning swallow, as in the bird), in the general vicinity of today's Beijing. Yan was famed for its wild fruits and berries as well as for supplying the Shang rulers with white horses and good wives. The state of Zhou conquered the Shang in approximately 1000 BCE. Zhou organized its kingdom into fiefdoms: the one they called Northern Yan was right where it all started with Peking Man, in today's Fangshan county.

Close by was a small walled city called Ji, named after a type of thistle. Ji was urban Beijing's first true ancestor. In a canal-side park by today's Guang'anmen overpass in the city's southwest, a small monument commemorates over 3,000 years of continuous history as a city (or a progression of cities) on that spot. Yan eventually annexed Ji to become one of the dominant Warring States of the tumultuous Eastern Zhou period (722–221 BCE).

Ji flourished within Yan, becoming one of the most celebrated cities of the era. On market days, farmers brought in live chickens, sheep, pigs and produce from their iron-ploughed fields. Nomadic tribesmen from across the Yanshan Mountains to the north, the ancestors of today's Mongols and Manchus, galloped into town to trade horses and carpets for grain, salt, dates, pottery, meat and cloth. They also introduced stringed instruments and musical traditions that the locals blended with their own.

Yet corruption and nepotism nipped at the heels of prosperity. The annals of Yan celebrate good King Zhao, who was so determined to stem the rot that he had miscreants disembowelled or cut in half. He built a magnificent Golden Tower east of the city to celebrate a great teacher and welcome more upright men to his kingdom. Yan grew strong once more. King Zhao's well-fed army, high in morale, fought many a successful campaign against Yan's rivals.

After King Zhao's death, standards slipped. Officials imposed heavy taxes on the people to support an army that they no longer fed so well, while feasting grandly themselves. When Yan suffered a string of military defeats, the nomadic tribes of the north, sniffing weakness, stopped trading and began raiding. Even the 650 km of fortifications that Yan hastily threw up along its northern border – among the earliest of what should properly be called China's 'Great Walls' – failed to halt the pillage. In 222 BCE the rival state of Qin, based in the west, conquered Yan and seized Ji.

The Qin ruler, the legendary tyrant Qinshihuang, became the first emperor to unify all China; his capital was in what we now call Xi'an. As Ji sat at the junction of two strategic new roads, he made it a military command centre. Qinshihuang continued the work of fortifying the northern borders, not just at Ji, but from the sea in the east all the way to Central Asia. The footprints of the Qin Great Walls – a discontinuous chain of tamped-earth walls, watchtowers, signal towers and forts – remain: I was once visiting a Beijing real estate mogul in her resort-scale weekender in the hills north of the city when she casually pointed out the remains of a Qin era Great Wall crowning a ridge on her property.

When Qinshihuang died, the empire disintegrated. Ji became part of a revived Kingdom of Yan. Irrigators tapped the Yongding and Gaoliang rivers to the city's north and farming flourished.

Monument to Three Millennia of Urban History at Guang'anmen.

Ji grew famed again for the excellence of its fruit, dates and chestnuts as well as its sericulture and the sweetness of its wells. But by the fourth century BCE corruption, along with rebellion, banditry, nomadic raids and a plague of locusts, reduced this prosperous city to a burned-out and depopulated wasteland. Ji's fortunes rose and fell numerous times over the next two centuries until, in 581, the Sui dynasty managed to unify China once more.

The Sui made Ji part of an administrative prefecture they called Youzhou. The new regime press-ganged more than a million men to continue the work of building the Great Walls as well as roads, granaries and supply lines for their armies. Five million more achieved the monumental feat of digging the Grand Canal that connected the Yellow, Yangtze, Qiantang and Huai rivers, linking Ji directly with the wealthy southern city of Hangzhou. Ji grew secure and prosperous once more. Its population soared to 100,000. And yet the continuing pressures of corvée labour and high taxes in all parts of the empire pushed people once more into poverty, banditry and rebellion. In 624 the Sui fell and the golden age of the Tang dynasty began.

The Tang, which had its capital in today's Xi'an, turned Youzhou into a military base from which to mount expeditions against the increasingly belligerent northern tribes. Buddhism was not unknown in China before the Tang and the first Chinese translations of Buddhist texts had appeared four centuries earlier. But the legendary pilgrimage of the monk Xuanzang, who travelled the Silk Road to India, returning with 22 horses laden with scriptures, icons and other Buddhist miscellany (an odyssey immortalized in the novel *Journey to the West*, on which the popular 'Monkey' stories are based), led to its popularization. Fittingly, Beijing's earliest Buddhist temple dates from this time. It was called the Minzhong (Mourning the Loyal) Temple, in honour of soldiers fallen in the northern campaigns, specifically that against the Korean kingdom of Goguryeo. An ornamental stone pillar just south of the Fayuan (Source of the Law) Temple, in Beijing's Xuanwu District, marks the site of the original buildings of the Minzhong Temple. These had been destroyed, over the course of centuries, by war, fire and earthquakes. Another Beijing Buddhist temple with antecedents in the Tang is the Wofo (Reclining Buddha) Temple in the Western Hills. Beijing's largest temple devoted to China's native philosophy-cum-religion of Daoism (sometimes spelled Taoism in English), Baiyun Guan (White Cloud Temple), also dates back to this era.

Even the glorious Tang eventually fell into the trap of misrule and rebellion. In the century and a half between 763 and 934, Youzhou changed hands 28 times. If King Zhao is ancient Beijing's most fondly recalled ruler, its most hated dates to this time. The Tang warlord Liu Rengong (r. 895–914) forced his subjects to trade in their copper coins for ones of iron and clay, conscripted every man between the ages of 15 and 70 into his army, and even banned the importation of tea from the south so that people had to buy the inferior local herb over which he enjoyed a monopoly. His own son overthrew him and another warlord killed them both.

In 938 the Buddhist Khitan people, who ultimately vanquished the Tang, took the city. Related to the Mongols, the Khitans readily assimilated people of other ethnicities into their ranks. While preserving aspects of their own culture such as male–female egalitarianism, they happily adopted useful aspects of Chinese culture and governance. Having grown strong and rich controlling trade along the Silk Road, they were so well known among nations that even today, the Russians use the word *kitaitsy* to mean Chinese. Cathay, medieval Europe's name for China, is a variant of Khitay. Declaring the founding of the Greater Liao (Boundless) dynasty in 947, the Khitans renamed the city Nanjing, or 'southern capital' – which, from the perspective of people from the far north, it was. Although Nanjing was only one of the Liao's five capitals, it was the largest and most populous.

But the Liao hadn't managed to conquer all of China. In 979, the rival southern-based Song dynasty dispatched an army of 300,000 northwards to take the city. The brave and capable Liao Empress Dowager Xiao Chuo commanded the Khitan army that drove back the Song; she eventually enforced a treaty that heralded a century of peace. Xiao Chuo's considerable legacy also included the introduction of civil service examinations, a ban on the murder of slaves and significant tax reform.

Monument marking the original site of the Minzhong Temple.

Buddhist monk in 'mobile' meditation at Fayuan Temple

GOOD FAITH

The Daoists tell the story of a (most likely apocryphal) meeting between Confucius (551–479 BCE) and the founder of philosophical Daoism, Lao Zi (dates uncertain – probably lived sometime between 604 and 471 BCE). Confucius began to explain his ideas, which centre on the notion of moral governance from the state down through to the family. Interrupting, Lao Zi told him to get to the point. Confucius replied: 'goodness and duty'. Were these, Lao Zi asked, 'qualities natural to man'? Confucius said they were. If man learned to follow the natural course, or *Dao*, Lao Zi replied, 'you will no longer need to go round laboriously advertising goodness and duty, like the town-crier with his drum, seeking for news of a lost child.'

No self-respecting Daoist would work for government, but no self-respecting Confucian would give up trying for the job. Confucianism has informed the philosophy and rituals of governance in China from ancient times; even the Communists embrace it today. Beijing's stately Confucian Temple, which dates back to the time of Khubilai Khan, is the second-largest in the country after that found in Confucius's home town of Qufu in Shandong province. Beijing's largest and most ancient Daoist temple, the sublime Baiyun Guan (White Cloud Temple), meanwhile, is home to China's Daoism Association and a few dozen blue-robed, top-knotted monks.

Historically, the majority of Beijing's temples have been Buddhist, including, as in the case of the Lama Temple, the Tibetan-Mongolian variant known as Lamaism. The city's biggest mosque, on Niu Jie in the city's southwest, dates back to 996 CE, and its earliest Nestorian Christian monument to the fourteenth century. In Maoist times, all religions were condemned as 'superstition' (except worship of Mao himself). Today, anything goes – except cults with anti-Communist overtones (Falun Gong), religions aligned with a foreign power (Roman Catholicism), 'unregistered' churches and evangelicals, for atheists have the right to practise their non-beliefs without harassment.

In 1012 the Liao renamed the city again, calling it Yanjing (Capital of Swallows). Another cycle of prosperity began and its people prayed for the good times to continue at a growing number of Buddhist temples. One, the Tianning, featured a 60-m-tall brick pagoda that even now stands sentinel in the city's southwest, just north of Guang'anmen. A Muslim community settled in the neighbourhood of what is still called Niu Jie (Ox Street), building a mosque that, many times redeveloped, serves the community to this day.

Prayers couldn't stop the Jurchens, however, another ambitious northern tribe. For a while, the Jurchens paid tribute to the Liao. But legend has it that in 1112, when the Liao emperor demanded the Jurchen chieftain Aguta dance for his entertainment, he refused. When Aguta galloped up to the walls of Yanjing at the head of his army, the citizens threw open the gates rather than endure a siege. In 1115, Aguta declared himself emperor of the new Jin (Gold) dynasty. Just over a decade later, the Jurchens rode south and burned most of the towns in the southeast of China to the ground.

The Jurchens renamed Yanjing Zhongdu (Central Capital), and made it the seat of their empire in 1153. They expanded the walled city to about 5 km in circumference and banished some 30,000 potentially rebellious households to the south of the city walls.

In 1179 Aguta's grandson, the Shizong emperor, bequeathed to the city one of its most beloved features: its lakes, outside what were then the city walls to the northeast. He had an island constructed in the centre of Taiye Pond (today's Beihai, or North Lake) and called it Qionghua Dao (known in English as Hortensia Isle). There he built what became his favourite *xinggong*, 'detached palace', or palace away from the palace. Like the Khitans, the Jurchens acquired some Chinese cultural tastes; in the case of the Shizong emperor, for the unusually shaped and weathered stones in formations called *jiashan*, 'artificial mountains', that are a trademark of Chinese garden design. When Shizong sacked the Song capital of Kaifeng, he had his troops souvenir the Song emperor's considerable collection. These found a permanent home on Hortensia

Detail of the Marco Polo Bridge today.

Isle. Later emperors of the Jin grew so fond of the detached palace on Hortensia Isle that they stayed there from March through to August every year.

Shizong was also enamoured of Xiang Shan (Fragrant Mountain) and Yuquan Shan (Jade Spring Mountain) to the city's northwest, building pleasances and temples in the hills. He constructed the famous 'water garden', Diaoyutai (Fishing Terrace), south of the marshlands of Haidian. As the population grew, hydrologists built on the foundations of the Sui irrigation works, tapping the Jade Spring and other new sources of water for farmland. The Jin engineers also constructed the magnificent marble bridge spanning the Lugou River that's known in English today as the Marco Polo Bridge.

Genghis Khan, born Temujin (1162–1227).

In April 1214, less than 100 years after the Jurchens expelled the Khitans, Genghis Khan came knocking at the gates. By then, Zhongdu had a population of 1 million residing in 250,000 households; its palaces and many of its buildings were among the finest of their time.

Genghis Khan had a well-deserved reputation for fierceness. It's said that when one of his warriors suggested that falconry was life's greatest pleasure, Genghis Khan averred that better still was the act of vanquishing one's enemies, seizing their horses and possessions and ravishing their 'weeping women'. It took a mighty bribe of 3,000 horses, 1,000 young men and women (undoubtedly weeping), mounds of gold, hoards of silver, reams of silk, and one exceptionally beautiful princess, the daughter of the Jin Emperor, to persuade the Great Khan to leave the city in peace. One year later, he was back for a bout of 'glorious slaughter'. He left the streets running with blood and the prized palaces of the Jin reduced to ash and rubble.

2 Khanbalik

Europeans who experienced the sanguinary depredations of Genghis Khan's cavalry called the Mongols 'Tartars' and their realm 'Tartary' after Tartarus, the hell of Greek mythology. The Chinese considered them barbarians. Yet it was Khubilai Khan, Genghis's grandson, who created Beijing's most legendary incarnation, Khanbalik (City of the Khan).

By 1260 the Mongol realm stretched from Korea to eastern Europe. In 1271 Khubilai, inheriting the Chinese portion of the realm, established the Yuan (Original) dynasty. He would build his capital at Zhongdu. A Khitan man called Yelu Chucai, whose father had served the Jurchen Jin dynasty, had persuaded both Genghis Khan and his son and successor Ögedei that their Chinese subjects were more useful – and taxable – alive than dead, and that the Chinese system of governance that both the Liao and Jin had adopted was a sound one.

Khubilai also benefited from advice given to him by his mother, Sorghaghtani Beki. She was herself one of the towering figures of her age. She won the praise of poets, missionaries, historians and scholars from many lands; the great Syriac scholar Bar Hebraeus said of her: 'If I were to see among the race of women another woman like this, I should say that the race of women was far superior to that of men.' For a time, Sorghaghtani Beki administered parts of the Mongol empire including some of what is now Hebei Province; she passed on to her son valuable insights on how best to rule an agricultural people.

For the design of his capital, Khubilai turned to yet another adviser, the Chinese Buddhist monk Zicong. Zicong had authored a treatise on feng shui, Chinese geomancy, titled

Statue of Khubilai Khan in the Yuan Dynasty Relics Park.

The Canon of the Jade Ruler. Zicong was also an authority on ancient Confucian and Daoist texts including the I Ching (Book of Changes). The 63-year-old polymath had already designed one fabled city for the Khan. When, to quote Coleridge, 'in Xanadu, did Kubla Khan / A stately pleasure-dome decree', he had decreed it from Zicong.

Now Zicong was to design Khanbalik, or as it was known in Chinese, Dadu (Great Capital), in accordance with an extension of feng shui that Hok-Lam Chan, the author of *Legends of the Building of Old Peking*, calls 'astral geography'. This ancient form of urban planning was based on the notion that the emperor was to his court and domain as the Pole Star was to the constellations. If the earthly realm reflected the celestial order, then ruler and ruled would enjoy peace, stability and prosperity. By situating the ruler's palace within three concentric sets of walls, one for the palace itself, one for the Imperial Precinct enclosing it and one for the city as a whole – the number three suggesting heaven, earth and humankind – the scheme places the emperor at the symbolic nucleus of the universe. These principles guided the layout of the canal city Suzhou, the Tang capital Chang'an (Xi'an) and the Han dynasty's Luoyang. In Khanbalik, they reached their supreme expression.

The Jurchens' palace had not even given a cursory nod to the principles of feng shui. Its central axis ran east–west, not north–south. It had neither mountains at the back to block the flow of negative yin, nor slow-flowing water and a clear view to the south to encourage positive yang. The Yuan would have to start from scratch.

Augurs foretold that if Khanbalik were constructed on the exact site of Zhongdu, rebellion would follow. The feng shui of the area to the immediate northeast, however, was superb: like a 'coiling dragon, crouching tiger'. As for the precise location of the palace, Zicong credited the guidance of a tree just south of today's Tiananmen; Khubilai gave the tree the rank of 'general' and hung lanterns on its branches at festival time.

By 1276 nearly 30 km of tall, tapering tamped-earth walls had risen around the new, nearly square city. Under the bright northern sun they shone yoghurt-white like the Mongol yurts; whereas for Chinese, white was the colour of mourning, for Mongols it signified celebration and nobility. Nine guarded, gleaming red gates pierced the white walls. Attached to each was a specialized storeroom holding quivers, saddles, bridles or other equipment for the Mongol cavalry.

Fifty is a significant number in the I Ching. Zicong gave the city 50 square residential, administrative and commercial wards. Nine straight north–south and east–west avenues, each about 36 m wide, broad enough for nine chariots to travel side by side, gridded the city. The minor streets were half as wide. Then there were 29 east–west *hutong*, residential alleyways, which, at 6–7 m across, were half as wide again as the smaller streets. Khanbalik's precise geometry was only broken in elegant accommodation of the Jin dynasty lakes, now enclosed within the city itself and, in the case of Beihai (North Lake) and Zhonghai (Central Lake), inside the walled Imperial Precinct.

The grey-walled *hutong,* and the courtyard homes known as *siheyuan* that they contain, are residential Beijing's most emblematic features. The word *hutong* only occurs in Beijing and its immediate environs. It is a loanword from Mongolian and other central Asian languages, and most likely means a drinking well; all the first *hutong* were lanes with wells. According to the linguist Zhang Qingchang, it was originally pronounced 'huto'. Eight different ways of transcribing the sound in Chinese characters were eventually unified into the current one (胡同). The first documented reference to *hutong* in the Chinese language is the Yuan dynasty play *Zhang sheng zhu hai* (*Zhang Sheng Boils the Sea*) by Li Haogu, in which one character asks 'Where can I find you?' and another answers, 'Zhuanta Hutong', Brick Pagoda Hutong – which can still be found just west of today's commercial street Xidan.

In 1285 the former residents of Zhongdu began moving into Khanbalik. First in were the elites, who were allocated the most desirable properties. By 1290, Khanbalik was the grandest capital of any Chinese dynasty to its time and among the finest cities in the world. Its most famous chronicler, the Venetian traveller Marco Polo, wrote of 'Cambulac' with awe:

> The streets are so straight and wide that you can see right along them from end to end and from one gate to the other . . . the whole city is arranged in squares just like a chessboard.

When asked for directions, the people of Beijing, even now, tend to give directions by referring to the points of the compass, east, west, north or south, rather than right or left. Marco Polo described how these avenues were lined with trees that provided shade in summer and, in winter storms, helped travellers find their way. He marvelled at the many grand buildings, fine homes, inns, shops and temples as well as specialist markets for gems and geese, camels and hats.

Post roads ribboned out from the city gates. The Mongols' pony express was so fast and efficient that, according to a later visitor from Venice, the Catholic missionary Odoric de Pordenone, 'the Grand Khan receives news in twenty-four hours from countries at a distance of at least three days' ordinary riding'. Vibrant suburbs sprang up along the post roads. They encompassed markets of their own, caravanserais housing great crowds of travellers, merchants and ambassadors, and brothels staffed by tens of thousands of prostitutes. Khanbalik's suburban population at times equalled that of the city itself: some half a million by the end of the thirteenth century.

Khubilai charged a Chinese hydrologist called Guo Shoujing with reconstructing the Grand Canal of the Sui dynasty, by then in ruins. Diverting water from the Jade Stream in the Western Hills, Guo repaired, re-routed and shortened the canal. He devised an ingenious system of 24 locks. These allowed barges pulled by teams of peasants all the way from Hangzhou, and loaded with southern goods and foodstuffs, to dock at Jishuitan (Collecting Water Pool) where, Marco Polo attested, they received a raucous welcome of gongs and drums. Guo also created a reservoir for the waters of the Jade Spring, known today as Kunming Lake (on the grounds of the Summer Palace). The Khitan adviser Yelu Chucai was buried on the shore of the lake, where a small temple to his memory still stands. Only at the turn of the twentieth century did railways and shipping render Guo's hydraulics obsolete.

Of all the wonders of Khanbalik, none matched the Khan's palace – according to Marco Polo, 'the greatest palace that ever was'. Its single-storey buildings were crowned with 'lofty' roofs, their walls 'all covered with gold and silver' and decorated with gilt dragons, 'beasts and birds, knights and gods'. It featured marble stairways and a hall 'so large that it could easily dine 6,000 people'. Marco Polo wrote:

> The building is altogether so vast, so rich, and so beautiful, that no man on earth could design anything superior to it. The outside of the roof is all [coloured] with vermilion and

The Yuan dynasty reservoir Kunming Lake today (part of the Summer Palace).

yellow and green and blue and other [colours], which are fixed with a varnish so fine and exquisite that they shine like crystal . . .

Among the innumerable treasures of the palace was a gold and pearl-studded clepsydra, a water clock, with a golden figurine that announced the hour with placards.

Parklands recreated the wild landscape of the Mongolian steppes and complemented the architectural grandeur of the

palace. Ducks, geese and swans swam in the lakes, including Taiye Pond (today's Beihai). Wildflowers of Mongolian blue bloomed on their shores, and white stags, gazelles and roebucks grazed under fruiting trees. The lake itself was stocked with all varieties of fish for the emperor's table, prevented by metal grates from escaping to the rivers that fed into and flowed out of the lake.

On the Jin dynasty Hortensia Isle, Khubilai Khan built an artificial hill, Green Mount, of which Marco Polo reported:

Foreigners picnicking on Beijing's city walls, 1919.

EXOTICA

Marco Polo tells us that at Khubilai Khan's great banquets, Mongolian barons helped 'foreigners, who do not know the customs of the Court', from committing such literal faux pas as stepping on the raised threshold when entering (an act punishable by a beating).

The Khan's successors didn't make it so easy for foreigners in Beijing to cross that threshold. Jesuits squeaked into the Ming and Qing courts only because they possessed knowledge the court found useful. It took an unequal treaty forced on the Qing in 1844 to legalize teaching Chinese to foreigners and another to sanction their residence in Beijing.

By the time the Australian George Ernest Morrison ('G. E.' or 'Chinese' Morrison) arrived as correspondent for the London *Times* in 1897, imperialism had forced open China's doors, but at the price of China's humiliation. In 1949 Mao shut those doors on all but Communism's fellow travellers. Thirty years later Deng opened them once more, but on China's terms.

Today, nearly 200,000 foreigners reside in Beijing, 70,000 of them students. Despite the conspicuousness of those of non-Asian background, the majority hail from other Asian countries.

Wangfujing was briefly named Morrison Street in English after the Australian, but foreigners rarely leave as much of an impression on Beijing as it leaves on them. The exceptions are those who have treated it badly, from the French and British who sacked the Yuanmingyuan in 1860 to the British man in 2012 whose drunken harassment of a Chinese woman led to his beating and viral shaming on the internet.

Marco Polo wrote of the threshold rule that guests were 'not expected to stick at this in going forth again, for at that time some are like to be the worse for liquor, and incapable of looking to their steps'. These days, the expectation is that they'd better do so.

wherever a beautiful tree may exist, and the emperor gets news of it, he sends for it and has it transported with all its roots and the earth attached to them, and planted on that hill of his. No matter how big the tree may be, he gets it carried by his elephants; and in this way he has got together the most beautiful collection of trees in the whole world. He has also ordered the whole hill to be covered with green stones. Thus not only are the trees all green, but the hill itself is all green likewise; and there is nothing to be seen on it that is not green; and hence it is rightly called the Green Mount. On top of the hill there is another fine big palace which is all green inside and out. Thus, the hill, the trees, and the palace form together a charming spectacle.

The 'fine big palace' was Khubilai's legendary 'detached palace', the Jade Palace. The Khan and his guests reached the isle by crossing a bridge, described by Odoric as 'the finest that I have ever seen, both for the quality of the marble and for the delicacy of architecture.' A Muslim architect had designed the Jade Palace complete with mechanical fountains, Turkish baths with perfumed waters and a special Rouge and Powder Pavilion where the women could freshen up. The Jade Palace was the site of endless amusements: mechanical dancing peacocks, viewings of caged beasts and feasts for up to 600 people. Men and women drank wine in golden goblets refreshed from golden pitchers or dipped into an enormous carved black jade bowl that, Marco Polo tells us, '[exceeded] the value of four great towns' and that was emptied 'by the riotous crowd of revellers as fast as pipes could bring the liquor flowing into it'. Jugglers, magicians and musicians entertained the guests until everyone was 'full of laughter and enjoyment'.

On other occasions, colourful 'dragon barges' with moving tails and fins carried jolly imperial parties over the crystal waters of the lake to opera stages and wine shops nestled in the shade of pines, junipers and willows. The Khan and his court didn't neglect to provide spectacles for the common people, either. His grand imperial processions included one at New Year led by 500 splendidly adorned elephants. Even the ritual washing

Khubilai Khan's 'Green Mount' today: Hortensia Isle in Beihai Park.

of the elephants in the moat outside the city walls on the sixth day of the sixth month was part of the pageantry of daily life in Khanbalik.

Under Khubilai's patronage, crafts, science, medicine and astronomy flourished in the capital, benefiting from the talents of a diverse population that included not only Mongols and Chinese, but Uighurs and others from the Central Asian deserts, Europe and the Middle East. People of all religions were welcome: Khubilai's own mother, Sorghaghtani Beki, was a Nestorian Christian. It was to her credit that Khubilai was religiously tolerant, literate and respectful of Chinese tradition – all attributes that benefited both Khanbalik and its residents.

Khubilai's grandson and successor Temur Khan (r. 1294–1307) would continue the tradition of religious tolerance, welcoming to Khanbalik a papal envoy, Franciscan friar John de Montecorvino. The friar built two churches in the city and claimed to have baptized 'more than ten thousand Tartars', converting several prominent Nestorians to Catholicism in the process.

Khubilai Khan was mindful of the high place of Confucianism in Chinese culture and society. This philosophy holds that

Beijing's Confucian Temple, which dates back to the time of Khanbalik.

Detail of stela at the Confucian Temple.

a ruler's authority is based on moral example and the advice of scholar-officials, chosen for service in the court through competitive examinations. Khubilai founded the magnificent and still extant Confucian Temple as well as the National College (Guozijian) next door, where Mongol boys studied Chinese and Chinese boys studied Mongolian. He added a state library to the complex in 1313. The temple became home to ten black stone drums acquired by the Jurchens when they sacked Kaifeng. The drums were believed to date back to the Zhou dynasty (1122–255 BCE); the hunting poems carved on them were among the earliest examples of Chinese writing. (The original drums were lost; the drums on exhibition at the Confucian Temple today are copies from the eighteenth-century reign of the Qianlong emperor.) Khubilai conscientiously performed Confucianist state rituals such as agricultural rites at the Altar to the God of Land and Grain (in today's Zhongshan Park adjoining the Forbidden City), and the cultivation of sesame, beans, melons and even rice in paddy-fields irrigated by the waters of Jishuitan.

Khubilai's second wife Chabi, renowned for her wise policy advice as well as the hat and robe designs that would define

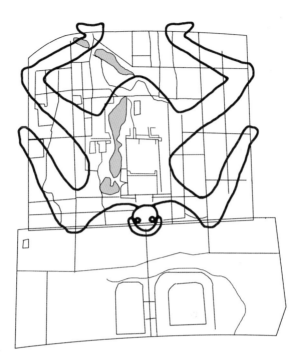

Image of Nezha superimposed on plan of the Ming dynasty capital Beijing.

Mongolian fashion for centuries, was an ardent devotee of Tibetan Buddhism; she even gave their first son the Tibetan name Dorghi. Khubilai restored some of the area's ancient Buddhist temples, commissioning a Nepali architect to rebuild the Liao dynasty White Dagoba; it still stands, 51 m tall, near the old city's southwest gate of Fuchengmen.

The city acquired its founding myth during Khubilai's rule. Nezha was a Tantric child deity, dharma enforcer and demon-battler with a breath of blue mist who could grow three heads and six arms at will. The story went that when Nezha bathed in the Eastern Sea, he accidentally trampled on the palace of the Dragon King, the ruler of the Bitter Sea Waste (North China Plain). In the battle for control over rain and water, Nezha slew all nine sons of the Dragon King, proving himself the perfect guardian spirit for a place subject to drowning rains and lengthy droughts. Nezha was a popular character in Yuan drama, and Khanbalik was nicknamed Nezha Town.

For all the kowtowing to Confucius, Mongol law still reserved its harshest punishments for ethnic Chinese. In practice, imperial appointments largely supplanted the civil service examinations that had historically afforded even the least advantaged the hope that they could elevate themselves and their family fortunes through study. Qualified Han Chinese scholars found themselves sidelined in favour of the Khan's fellow outlanders, as Persians, Turks and others took many of the plum positions at court.

Among these 'coloured-eye people' (*semu ren*), as they were known, was Khubilai's minister of finance, a man called Ahmed Benaketi from what is today Uzbekistan. Ahema, as he is commonly known, was corrupt and ruthless. In 1282 a 29-year-old Chinese resident of Khanbalik by the name of Wang Zhu smashed Ahema's skull with a bronze hammer. Khubilai and his court were in Xanadu when the news of Ahema's murder rippled through the city followed by unabashed jubilation as a citizenry long oppressed by Ahema's shameless, incessant taxation celebrated his demise. Khubilai ordered Wang Zhu captured and killed, but once he learned the truth, he exonerated his minister's murderer, albeit posthumously.

Khubilai died just over a decade after this event and his successors restored the civil service exams. Yet they continued to deny Han Chinese all but the lowest offices. Overeducated, underemployed and increasingly impoverished, some literati channelled their energy and discontent into writing plays, one reason the Yuan is known as a golden age for Chinese theatre. Wang Shifu's *Xixiang Ji* (*Romance of the Western Chamber*), a story of illicit love set in the Tang dynasty, is a Yuan classic that also provides early evidence of the *er* sound that Beijing people characteristically affix to the end of many words and compounds. Another famous play from that time, Guan Hanqing's *Gantian dongdi Dou E yuan* (*How the Injustice Done to Dou E Moved Heaven and Earth*) tells the story of a young widow framed for murder by a man she refuses to marry. The theme of a defenceless woman hounded to death by a powerful and corrupt man resonated with the Mongols' Chinese subjects.

Wary of insurrection, the Yuan rulers imposed a curfew on the city. Once the Bell Tower in the city centre had tolled three times, no one was to leave home. Anyone caught outside for any reason less than a medical emergency could look forward to seeing in the dawn under interrogation.

Legend has it that when the building of Khanbalik began, the first spadeful of earth that was turned unearthed a nest of red-headed worms. This spooked the monk Zicong, who saw them as an omen of dynastic collapse. Following Khubilai's death in 1294 the old patterns soon set in: corruption, infighting and rebellion. By 1368 the Yuan was on its eighth khan in just over seven decades. Natural disasters and epidemics, including a plague similar to the Black Death that the Mongols are believed to have taken to Europe, further doomed the dynasty.

In 1368 the Yuan dynasty was three years short of its centenary. A peasant rebel called Zhu Yuanzhang, at the head of an anti-Mongol army called the Red Turbans, stormed Khanbalik. The last Yuan emperor, Togan Timur, fled. Zhu Yuanzhang laid waste to the city that Togan Timur had called his 'bejewelled hearth' and declared himself the first emperor of the Ming dynasty.

3 The Ming Dynasty (1368–1644)

Zhu Yuanzhang set up the Ming court in warm, fertile central-south China, in a city he named Nanjing (Southern Capital – and which is still known by that name today). Though Nanjing would be safe from lightning raids by resurgent Yuan armies, the Mongol threat was still live. Beipingfu (Northern Peace Prefecture), as Khanbalik was now known, remained vital to the country's defence. Zhu named his fourth son, the ten-year-old Zhu Di, 'Prince of Yan' and dispatched him to the shattered, depopulated former capital in 1370 in the care of a trusted general, Xu Da.

To make the city easier to defend, Xu Da shrank it. He constructed a new northern boundary wall 2.9 km south of the old one while shifting the southern boundary further south by just under a kilometre to where today's Qianmen (Front Gate) stands. At about 30 sq. km, Beipingfu was two-thirds the size of Khanbalik.

The tamped-earth Yuan walls required constant maintenance and were vulnerable to attack. Xu Da faced the new walls with brick and topped them with crenellated ramparts. Beipingfu's city walls, 11 m high at their tallest, were wide and strong enough to support the movements of troops, horses and chariots. Whereas the Yuan city walls had nine gates, the Ming had seven. As the dynasty progressed, barbicans, arrow towers and enceintes would further fortify the walls and gates giving them an aesthetic form and solidity that lasted well into the twentieth century.

Zhu Di settled into a pied-à-terre of 811 rooms in the Khans' old palace, demolishing the rest. By the time his father died, 28 years later, the intelligent and ambitious Zhu Di was in his prime and commanded a loyal army of 50,000. When he learned that his bookish 21-year-old nephew was his father's chosen successor, Zhu Di was outraged. He rode south with his men. After three years of warfare against his nephew, the Jianwen emperor, he razed Jianwen's palace to the ground. Jianwen's body was never found. Zhu Di declared himself the Yongle (Perpetual Happiness) emperor and returned north.

In January 1403 Yongle gave Beipingfu the name Beijing (Northern Capital) and made it the seat of the Ming empire. To guarantee a food supply, he dispatched soldiers and convicts to work with peasants to cultivate the surrounding wilderness. They planted hardy grains such as millet, wheat, barley and sorghum alongside crops of turnips, carrots and cabbage. On barges pulled by hundreds of coolies up the newly restored Grand Canal came supplies from the south, including rare hardwoods for the building of a grand, new palace and imperial capital.

Yongle conscripted 1 million men to restore and construct more than 1,000 km of Great Walls snaking over the ranges north of the city, cutting off Mongol attack routes. Another million labourers, including 100,000 artisans, worked on the new palace.

Like that of Khubilai, Yongle's palace faced south, straddling a central north–south axis, the northern end of which was capped by Drum and Bell Towers (still standing today). The Ming situated their axis east of that of the Yuan so that, being closer to the rising sun, the Ming's qi (vital essence, or breath) would subdue that of the Yuan. Workers digging moats and expanding the lakes helped to bury the Yuan by heaping mud on to the ruins of the old palace. Soil from the moats and lakes also went into enlarging a hill created just north of the palace by the Yuan, today's Jingshan (Prospect Hill) Park. Jingshan is what feng shui theories call a *kaoshan*, or 'mountain to lean on'; it's complemented to the south by the Jinshui He (River of Golden Waters) that flows in graceful curves across the palace's forecourt.

As in the Yuan, the walled palace (later named Zijin Cheng, the Forbidden City) lay within the embrace of a walled Imperial Precinct encompassing lakes and parkland as well as the imperial Ancestral Temple and the Altar to the God of Land and Grain. The Imperial Precinct's southern entrance was the gate later named Tiananmen (Gate of Heavenly Peace). A T-shaped space backed up against the Imperial Precinct, its stem the north–south Corridor of a Thousand Steps, or Imperial Way, leading to the city wall's Qianmen (Front Gate), which was in perfect north–south alignment with the gates of the Imperial Precinct and the palace itself.

Further south, Yongle built the Temple of Heaven (Tiantan) and the Temple of the First Farmer (Xiannongtan). The original Hall of Prayer for Good Harvests in the Temple of Heaven was square, replaced only in 1545 by the now-iconic round hall with its three-tiered roof, then tiled in blue, gold and green. Other key imperial rites would be held at Ditan (Altar of the Earth) to the north, Ritan (Altar of the Sun) to the east and Yuetan (Altar of the Moon) to the west. The walled Imperial Precinct stretched from Ditan south to Tiananmen and from Dong'anmen (Gate of Eastern Peace) west to Xi'anmen (Gate of Western Peace).

The design of the palace that 24 emperors of two dynasties would call home combined the best features of Khubilai's palace and the one Yongle destroyed in Nanjing. The goal, as Geremie Barmé writes in *The Forbidden City*, was to 'create nothing less than a terrestrial refraction of the realm of the celestial Jade Emperor, or Heavenly Ancestor, and his court which was said to rule over the universe.'

The emperor's chief ceremonial hall, later called the Taihedian (Hall of Supreme Harmony), thus rested atop a marble ziggurat symbolizing the mountain at the centre of the universe in Buddhist cosmology. Within, his throne perched on another stepped platform, this one representing the nine layers of Heaven. The number nine, *jiu*, is a homonym of the Chinese character meaning 'everlasting'; it is associated with a high degree of yang (male, active) energy. Nine auspicious figures ride the flying eaves of the main halls (with the eccentric exception of the Taihedian, which has ten); the number nine figures in the dimensions of all the ceremonial buildings; and

Hall of Prayer for Good Harvests at the Temple of Heaven.

nine dragons dance across the magnificent ceramic screens
of the Forbidden City and Beihai Park.

An imperial quarry near Peking Man's old haunts at
Fangshan supplied the white marble for the Taihedian's
'cinnabar stairway stone', the ramp carved with five-toed
imperial dragons over which the emperor was carried in
his golden palanquin into the hall. It took 1,000 horses
and mules to haul the stone to the palace in winter along
a throw rug of ice created by splashing water onto the road.

The kilns at Liulichang (Glazed Tile Factory), south of the
walled city, produced the ceramic tiles for the palace, including
the mustard-gold roofing tiles used exclusively for palace roofs.
The imperial library was the only palace building roofed in
black because, as the colour geomantically associated with
water, it was a talismanic precaution against fire.

Within the palace, civil officials occupied the offices to
the east of the imperial halls – the east evoking wood, spring

and growth. The military occupied the west – metal, autumn and force. Everything had its place, even dissent: the *huabiao*, decorative winged pillars with dragons' bodies and lions' heads standing sentinel at Tiananmen, invited senior officials to criticize the emperor should he stray from the path of virtue.

Because of their association with masculine yang, odd numbers featured in the dimensions of all the halls of government. The buildings in the northern, residential part of the palace, where the women of the seraglio lived and which was forbidden to all men except the emperor and eunuchs, were linked to the feminine yin principle, and built with even-numbered dimensions. These were designed, in Barmé's words, for 'intimacy and intrigue rather than vistas

The Taihedian (Hall of Supreme Harmony) in the Forbidden City.

and spectacle'. They were lit by oil lamps and heated, in braziers and under the brick platform beds, by charcoal of such superior quality that it produced no smoke and burned down to fine, odour-absorbing ash that eunuchs used to line the emperor's platinum potty.

The palace also contained imperial workshops, places of worship and meditation, kitchens, pharmacies, libraries, tearooms, theatres, schools and armouries. It covered 72 ha and contained 9,999.5 rooms (so as not to presume on the perfection that was Heaven's alone).

The Ming city retained the chessboard design of the Yuan. But now there were more than 30 major north–south avenues, plus smaller streets, and 458 *hutong*, running largely east–west.

Forbidden City detail.

The east–west boulevard just south of Tiananmen was called Chang'an (Eternal Peace), after the much-admired capital of the Tang dynasty, today's Xi'an.

The preparations were finally complete. Yet the Ming court, still in Nanjing and accustomed to the refined pleasures and rice-bowl comforts of the south, grizzled at the thought of moving to the cold, dusty and hostile north. Making the case for Beijing, a group of scholar-officials collaborated on a sublime hand-scroll of poems, essays and paintings called *The Eight Views of Beijing.* 'Layered Shades of Green at Juyong Pass' and 'Dawn Moonlight at Lugou [Marco Polo] Bridge' portrayed the majestic defences of the Great Walls to the north and the famous Jin dynasty bridge in the south. 'Cascading Rainbow at Jade Stream Mountain' illustrated Beijing's natural beauty (and, pointedly, water supply) while 'Crystal Clear Waves at Taiye Pond' and 'Spring Clouds at Hortensia Isle' celebrated its man-made wonders. 'Sunset on the Golden Tower' alluded to the glorious days of King Zhao, 'Misty Trees at Jimen' evoked the bustling grandeur of Zhongdu and 'Clearing Snow on West Mountain' the area's rustic beauty.

When they finally shlepped north in 1421, the courtiers' misgivings were reinforced by the sight of refugees fleeing south from famine. Three months later, lightning struck the palace, reducing three halls to ashes. Some ventured that it was a sign of Heaven's displeasure. Yongle threw his critics in prison and began rebuilding.

Within the city, official rank dictated the number and size of rooms and courtyards a person could have in his home. Imperial regulations prescribed the colours with which people could decorate and even the exact depth of the entryway – the higher the status, the deeper the door. To flaunt any of these rules was to invite the death penalty.

Though Yongle employed Mongols in his army he forbade the speaking of Mongolian within the city and barred Mongolian fashions from Beijing. As the capital of a Chinese dynasty, with a predominantly Chinese population, the hybrid Beijing vernacular absorbed more words, phrases and linguistic habits from other Chinese dialects than ever before.

After Yongle died leading a campaign against the Mongols in 1424, his son and successor led the relieved court back to Nanjing. It took over ten years and another two brief imperial reigns before Beijing was once more the Ming capital. Only in 1441 did the government ministries ranged to either side of the Imperial Way (military to the west, civil to the east) finally remove the preface *xingzai* (residence *pro tempore*) from their signboards.

Early in his reign, on the eve of a hunting trip, Yongle had asked a trusted general, Gang Bing, to guard the palace women in his absence. Returning, he heard rumours that Gang had disported himself in the harem. Yongle confronted Gang, who produced a bag from the emperor's own saddlery. It contained the general's severed genitalia: foreseeing the opportunity for trouble-making on the part of his enemies, Gang secretly castrated himself before Yongle's departure. Yongle richly rewarded Gang for such above-and-beyond loyalty. When Gang died in 1410, Yongle endowed an ancestral hall in the western outskirts in his honour; it became known as the Eunuchs' Temple.

Eunuchs usually came from poor families. Their parents had them castrated in the hope that as servants of the palace, they'd lift the family fortunes. Yongle's father perceived that eunuchs' proximity to power and the fact that there was little other reward for their sacrifice made them prone to influence peddling and other self-enriching mischief. So he banned eunuchs from both political participation and the Confucian education that was the recognized and legitimate key to power. He restricted them to menial tasks, the 'cleaning and sweeping' of the palace residences.

The Xuande emperor (r. 1425–35) naively established a school for eunuchs within the palace itself and entrusted them to supervise both politics and military affairs. Eunuchs rapidly expanded in number and influence, 'cleaning and sweeping' their way through the treasury and causing a succession of political and financial scandals. While most spent long days in menial labour and short lonely nights in tiny cells within the palace, others accumulated obscenely large fortunes. According to *The Forbidden City*, one of the most egregiously corrupt, Liu Jin, acquired, among other things, two solid-gold suits of armour, thousands of gold rings and more than 11 kg of precious gems. Among the most controversial was Wang Zhen, who had tutored the Zhengtong emperor (r. 1435–49) as a child, and by the 1440s was considered the most powerful man in China.

Though much despised, Wang Zhen did leave Beijing a tangible legacy – the Zhihua Temple, the greatest extant example of Ming temple architecture in the city. Eunuchs patronized, funded and looked after the upkeep of hundreds of Buddhist temples, shrines and monasteries in Beijing and the surrounding hills. Confucianism, which placed supreme value on the continuation of one's family line through the production of male heirs, was not eunuch-friendly (nor did it approve, for similar reasons, of monastic celibacy). By contrast, the Buddhist doctrine of reincarnation offered eunuchs hope for reunion in the next life with their carefully preserved 'precious', kept ever-handy in a special jar.

The Ming saw a great flourishing of religion generally, with the establishment of over 1,000 Buddhist, Lamaist and Daoist temples as well as mosques, in Chinese, Mongolian, Tibetan, Uighur, Indian and Korean architectural styles. There were also many temples dedicated to specific deities – the City God, and the gods of war, literature and horses for example. There were temples just for opera singers and even for people with sick pets. The Chinese approach to religion has long tended towards inclusivity: laymen may burn joss at a Buddhist temple one day and at a Daoist temple the next, while carefully maintaining the altar to their ancestors that is at the heart of personal Confucian ritual.

In 1449 Wang Zhen convinced the Zhengtong emperor to lead what proved a disastrous campaign against the Mongols. The emperor was abducted and Wang Zhen himself killed. This prompted a succession crisis that concluded with the emperor's 21-year-old brother taking the throne as the Jingtai emperor.

Zhengtong returned eight years later and wrested back the throne. But the short-reigning Jingtai emperor made his own contribution to Beijing culture: he had such a fondness for blue *cloisonné* in particular that he invited Byzantine craftsmen to the capital to produce it for him; to this day, *cloisonné* is a Beijing speciality, known in Chinese (whatever its colour or date of origin) as *Jingtailan*, or 'Jingtai indigo'.

Other artisans who had come to furnish and decorate the palace helped make Ming Beijing a shoppers' paradise. The grand avenue east of the palace known then as the Street of the Ten Princely Residences (later Wangfujing, literally the Well of the Princely Residences) was renowned for its imperial supply shops. But the real action was in the southern suburbs outside Qianmen, where merchants who'd travelled north on the Grand Canal settled; the hundreds of new *hutong* there were named for their resident trade guild (Jade Polishing, for example), master craftsman (Coffin-maker Shang) or product (Beancurd, Hairpin,

Horse Post). Here too were the famous *langfang sitiao* (Gallery Streets), stately rows of carved and gilded shopfronts.

Shoppers could find fine silks from Hangzhou, porcelain from the imperial kiln at Jingdezhen and exotica such as leopard skins and ivory. As Timothy Brook notes in *The Confusions of Pleasure: Commerce and Culture in Ming China*, however, they needed to be well on guard against fakes and counterfeits: the fifteenth-century update of the early Ming shoppers' bible *Essential Criteria of Antiquities* advised that if you wanted properly made lacquer furniture with mother-of-pearl inlay in Beijing, you needed to have it made under supervision at home.

In the halcyon days of the Ming, foodstuffs were plentiful, whether imported from the south or locally grown. Specialized markets sold rice, fruit, vegetables – some cultivated in heated greenhouses – and livestock. As Jasper Becker observes in *The City of Heavenly Tranquility*, the citizens of fifteenth-century Beijing enjoyed a more varied diet than sixteenth-century Europeans. Eating out was popular and singers and storytellers entertained at the city's restaurants, teashops and taverns, sometimes with satirical poems and songs about corruption and official bastardry. (These days, sardonic political ditties are passed around by SMS or WeChat.)

Beijing's celebrated temple fairs date back to the Ming. They were carnivalesque affairs with stilt dancers, puppet shows, food, craft stalls and entertainment. Becker describes the astonishment of one visitor to the splendid New Year's Lantern Festival at Dengshikou (Lantern Market Crossroads) at seeing a eunuch pay 300 oz (19 lb; 8.5 kg) of silver for a lantern fashioned entirely of eggshells. At the time, a palace cook's monthly salary was about 2 oz (55 g) of silver; according to history scholars at Peking University, most workers lived on far less.

Not all eunuchs were a welcome sight to Beijing merchants. The city's most brutal standover gangs were composed of eunuchs who'd failed to enter palace service and were accepted nowhere else in society. The best policing efforts of the Imperial Brocaded Guards, whose most infamous chief got about in plainclothes on the back of a mule, could not stamp out crime.

A Beijing Spring Festival temple fair today.

The authorities installed lockable fences at the ends of the *hutong* throughout the area south of Qianmen that became known then as Dashila'r ('Big Fence' in Beijing patois).

Choe Bu, a 34-year-old Korean official shipwrecked in China, arrived in Beijing in 1488. As Becker writes, Choe Bu noted with distaste that while the 'Great Ming has washed off the old dirt and made those who buttoned their coats on the left [Mongols and Tibetans] take the ways of hat and gown' (and had thus 'civilized' them), the people worshipped Daoist and Buddhist gods. Even more repugnant to a stern Confucian such as himself, for whom scholars and farmers were the most respectable of social classes whereas only soldiers were lower than merchants, the people of Beijing preferred commerce to tilling the land. And worse still,

> Their clothing is short and tight, and men and women dress the same. Their food and drink are rancid . . . The

mountains, moreover are bare and the rivers filthy . . .
dust fills the sky.

Not in terms of population (about 700,000 at the time),
architecture or markets, he sniffed, did Beijing even 'come
close' to the civilized southern cities of Suzhou or Hangzhou.

By the time of Choe Bu's visit, the Ming was on its fifth
emperor after Yongle, the scholarly and upright Hongzhi
(*r.* 1487–1505), the only monogamous emperor in Chinese
history. Of similar temperament to Choe Bu, Hongzhi prose-
cuted the corrupt and curtailed the power of the eunuchs, efforts
wholly undone by his son, the hedonistic Zhengde (*r.* 1505–21).
Zhengde died childless despite having such an enormous harem
that the palace stores could scarcely feed them all.

The throne, again swarming with eunuchs, passed to
Zhengde's cousin, another reprobate: the Jiajing emperor.
In the wee hours of 27 November 1542, palace maids who'd
had enough of the emperor's sexual sadism were tightening
the ribbon around Jiajing's neck when their assassination
attempt was discovered. All were sentenced to the fearful
'death by a thousand cuts' (also known as 'slow slicing').
A shaken Jiajing quit the Forbidden City and moved with
his beloved cats Snow Brow and Tiger to the Lake Palaces at
Zhongnanhai (Central South Lakes), built within the Imperial
Precinct, just west of the Forbidden City on the foundations
of Khubilai's palace.

In 1550 the Mongol leader Altan Khan breached the Great
Walls and laid siege to the city. The defenders barred the
city gates with supports as thick as tree trunks. From atop
the walls, they fought off the invaders with firelocks, cannons
and arrows. Before withdrawing, Altan Khan looted and
burned the suburbs for three days. Jiajing considered building
a second city wall enclosing all the suburbs, but the cost was
prohibitive, so he walled in only the prosperous and densely
populated area south of Qianmen that included the Temple
of Heaven. This new wall, which had seven gates, was lower
and narrower than that of the main city. Together, the two

parts of the city wall, inner and outer, square and rectangle, took the shape of the Chinese ideograph for convex, 凸, and had a total circumference of 23.7 km. Beijing, now the largest capital city in the world, had almost three times as many streets as Khanbalik, including more than 450 *hutong*.

A truce with Altan Khan in 1571 gave the Ming a renewed lease of life. But Zhu Yuanzhang, the Ming founder, had promised a title and remuneration to all of his descendants. By the late sixteenth century tens of thousands of imperial clansmen were clamped to the imperial teat alongside an equal number of eunuchs and 3,000 palace women.

The righteous saw moral corruption everywhere, even in the undergarments of the merchants, who flaunted imperial law to wear silk, a luxury reserved for officials. Despite the ongoing ban on Mongol styles, as Antonia Finnane relates in *Changing Clothes in China*, Mongol-inspired, pleated-skirts called *yesa* became the fashionable Beijing man's must-have, while women wrapped themselves in chic Mongolian hooded cloaks. Another clothing fad, for Korean-style horse-tail skirts, Finnane writes, led to horses throughout the city losing their tails to thieving fashion victims.

As the 1580s drew to a close, the upright official Hai Rui, who'd escaped execution for remonstrating with Jiajing only because Jiajing died first, spoke out again. He urged the young Wanli emperor (r. 1572–1620) to punish the corrupt severely – by skinning embezzlers, for example, and stuffing their skin with straw for display. Wanli responded that such cruel punishment 'contradicts our sense of good government'.

Wanli's sense of good government didn't extend to worrying about the cruel punishments his own eunuch favourites inflicted on conscientious officials who dared oppose them. The most notorious eunuch of all, the vicious Wei Zhongxian, rode through the Forbidden City on his horse, an outrage to protocol. But even Wanli had his limits. When Wei refused to dismount in front of him, Wanli shot the horse from under Wei with an arrow.

At the age of 25, furious with his court for refusing to promote his beloved, Lady Zheng, to the rank of empress,

GREAT WALLS

The king has ordered [General] Nan-zhong
To build a fort on the frontier.
To bring out the great concourse of chariots,
With dragon banners and standards so bright.
The Son of Heaven has ordered us
To build a fort on that frontier.
Terrible is Nan-zhong;
The Xian-yun [people] are undone.

The frontier forts to which this poem from the sixth century BCE refers failed to 'undo' the Xianyun or any of the other militant tribes to China's north. The rulers of four out of the five dynasties that made Beijing their capital were nomadic tribes that had come conquering across these walls. As for the Xianyun (later called Xiongnü and possibly the ancestors of the Huns), they menaced Chinese states for nearly a thousand more years.

The Great Wall is in reality a series of discontinuous fortifications including walls, beacon stations and watchtowers stretching from China's northeast coast to its northwestern deserts. It came to symbolize China itself only after the Japanese occupied Manchuria in 1931; Mao was referring to the fight against the Japanese when in 1935 he wrote the famous line, 'Unless you make it to the Great Wall, you're no hero.' Richard Nixon became a hero in 1972 at Badaling and Pierre Cardin in 1979, when he launched his Spring/Summer collection there. Ravers have danced on it, artists have wrapped it and tourists, heroes all according to the souvenir t-shirt, stage daily human wave attacks on the ancient defences.

The great early twentieth-century writer Lu Xun called it 'a wonder and a curse', saying he felt 'hemmed in on all sides by the Great Wall'. The narrator of the popular Chinese television documentary miniseries *River Elegy* (1988) attacked it as

a symbol of confinement, conservatism, impotent defence, and timidity in the face of invasion. Because of its massive scale and venerable history, it has left the imprint of its grand conceit and self-deception on the very soul of the Chinese. Ah, Great Wall, why do we still sing your praises?

Great Wall near Beijing.

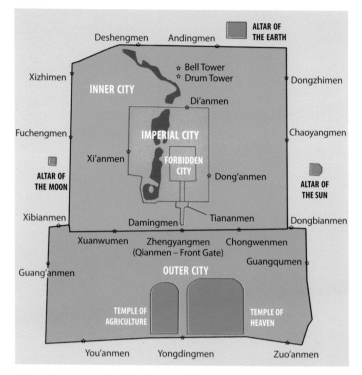

Schematic map showing Ming Inner and Outer Cities. The suffix 'men' means 'gate'.

Wanli effectively went on strike. He refused to attend court, banqueted his way to morbid obesity and spent the rest of his years constructing an opulent tomb for himself and Lady Zheng (at Dingling, in today's Changping county) so they would be united in the afterlife. Wanli was obsessed with tombs: he destroyed those of the Jin emperors and would have desecrated those of the Yuan as well but couldn't find them. No one ever has.

In 1602, when the Italian Jesuit Matteo Ricci, fluent in Chinese and trained in court etiquette, received permission to enter the Forbidden City, he kowtowed to an empty throne. Ricci was invited to stick around to teach the eunuchs how to wind the European clocks in the palace collection. He engaged in philosophical discussion with officials, drew maps of the world, taught eunuchs to play the harpsichord and devised the first system for transcribing Chinese into roman letters: Ricci's Latinate 'Pequim' gave us 'Peking'. As appalled by Beijing as Choe Bu had been, Ricci described the city as 'a true Babylon of confusion, full of every sort of sin, with no trace of justice or piety in anyone'. Its population was '*gente effeminate, deliziosa*' – effeminate and hedonistic. He estimated there were 40,000 prostitutes in Beijing including boys in ladies-of-the-night clothing.

In 1603, in response to an anonymous pamphlet attacking Lady Zheng, Wanli unleashed a wave of terror. Eunuchs tortured his critics at court and caned a famous Buddhist monk to death. Taxation and corruption reached intolerable levels. Coal miners protested. People starved. Bandits thrived. Peasant rebellions brewed. 'Purity', lamented one Chinese writer in 1609 (quoted by Brook in *The Confusions of Pleasure*), had been 'completely swept away and excess inundated the world'. The Jurchens, meanwhile, had established a new, improved Latter Jin dynasty north of the border. They became known as the Manchus. In 1636 their emperor, Nurhaci, changed the title of the dynasty to Qing (Clear).

A ruthless peasant rebel called Li Zicheng, who had killed hundreds of thousands of people by breaching the dykes of the Yellow River, reached Beijing with his army in early 1644 and laid siege to the city. The panicked Chongzhen emperor (r. 1628–44) murdered his wife, concubines and daughters to protect them from rape and hanged himself from a pavilion on Jingshan. The following morning, the people of Beijing awoke to find notices posted on every door proclaiming Li the emperor of a new dynasty.

As Li's army terrorized Beijing, over 300 km away, the Ming general Wu Sangui opened the Great Wall pass of Shanhaiguan to a Manchu-led army promising to help unseat the rebels. The Manchus did as promised: they drove Li out. Then they declared Beijing the capital of the Qing and put their six-year-old emperor Shunzhi on the throne.

Pictorial map of the Ming Tombs, after 1736, brush-and-ink watercolour.

4 The Qing Dynasty (1644–1911)

The Qing court rewarded Han Chinese who threw in their lot with the Manchus with government posts, land grants and inclusion in the Banners – the colour-coded Manchu military, political and social organization. In addition to Manchus and Han Chinese, the Banners also included many Mongols and even some Russians. The new rulers invited high-ranking Ming officials to serve the Qing and promised not to vandalize the Ming emperors' tombs. No one replaced General Wu at Shanhaiguan. The Great Walls, intended to keep out Manchus and Mongols, were allowed to fall to ruins.

Like the Mongols, the Manchus were great equestrians and hunters. They maintained imperial hunting grounds close to and within the city where the emperor could hunt wild boar, pheasants and even tigers, which were kept caged until needed. They were, however, content to maintain both the system of governance and architecture of Ming Beijing. Most changes were cosmetic: they rebuilt (and renamed) palace and other buildings that had been torched during the short but violent reign of Li Zicheng, and enhanced Beijing's parks and lakes. They gave Tiananmen its current name, and added Manchurian and sometimes Mongolian names to the signs on many palace and official buildings. Following a visit by the fifth Dalai Lama in 1651, the Qing court erected a Tibetan-style stupa – the White Dagoba – in his honour on Hortensia Isle, where Khubilai's Jade Palace once stood. (This is distinct from the Yuan era White Dagoba Temple to the west.)

The Manchu transformation of Beijing's human landscape was far more radical: in 1648 the emperor ordered all non-Bannermen Han Chinese out of the Inner City. Many migrated

The White Dagoba erected on Hortensia Isle at Beihai to honour the fifth Dalai Lama.

to Dashila'r (the Ming dynasty neighbourhood 'Big Fence') and other parts of the walled Outer City, which acquired the nickname 'the Chinese City'. Within the Inner City (later known in English as the 'Tartar City'), each Banner occupied a geographical quarter; Lanqiying (Blue Banner Camp) close to Peking University is just one place name that recalls those times.

Manchu directness, wit and manners contributed to the blend of roguishness, humour and courtesy that defines the archetypal Beijing personality. In humble courtyard houses and grand *wangfu* (princely mansions) alike, Manchus cultivated the leisure pursuits and *xiaowanyi'er* (little amusements) now spoken of as quintessentially Beijing: growing and tending courtyard gardens, making and flying kites and breeding crickets, goldfish and lapdogs, as well as art of constructing musical whistles to attach to the tail-feathers of homing pigeons, to mention a few.

Manchu men shaved the front of their heads and wore their hair long and plaited, hanging straight down the back like a horse's tail. The court ordered all Chinese men to do the same, on pain of death: no queue, no head. Manchu women, who wore their hair in high lacquered wings festooned with flowers and gems, enjoyed greater freedoms and social status than Chinese women and never bound their feet as Chinese women had done since the Tang dynasty. According to *The Manchu Way* by the Qing specialist Mark Elliott, many Chinese Bannerwomen eventually abandoned foot binding as well.

Wary of Ming restorationists, the court imposed a curfew on Beijing and policed the city heavily. More than 1,000 sentries kept watch from the walls, and the gates between the Inner and Outer Cities were shut between midnight and dawn. The Qing fortified Hortensia Isle with signal cannons and installed more than 1,700 lockable fences along the avenues and *hutong*. The Communist *hukou* (household registration) system harks back to the Qing, when it was decreed: 'Should there come [into the neighbourhood] an outsider, carefully check his history.' Even the fields close to the city walls were ploughed with furrows parallel to the walls to frustrate the advance of rebel cavalry.

The long-reigning Kangxi emperor (*r.* 1661–1722), one of the Qing's most exemplary rulers, tolerated only 400 eunuchs in his court, and strictly for 'cleaning and sweeping'. His harem was relatively modest as well: only 300 women. The conscientious Kangxi once penned an ode to a Western chiming clock. Jonathan Spence translated it in his brilliant 'autobiography' of Kangxi, *Emperor of China*:

> Red-capped watchmen, there's no need to announce dawn's coming.
> My golden clock has warned me of the time.
> By first light I am hard at work,
> And keep on asking, 'Why are the memorials late?'

Those imperial clock-winders, the Jesuits, won even greater favour with the Qing than the Ming. When the young German

Manchu women.

Jesuit Johann Adam Schall von Bell accurately predicted a
solar eclipse, the Shunzhi emperor (r. 1644–61) appointed
him head of the Bureau of Astronomy. After Schall von Bell
cured the emperor's sick mother with Western medicine, he
was permitted to build a cathedral, Nan Tang (Southern
Cathedral), inside Xuanwu Gate, on the site of Matteo
Ricci's old home.

Kangxi ordered all Jesuits to learn Manchu. He liked to
converse with them about cannons and windmills, cartography
and Euclidean geometry. They taught him to play the harpsichord. They never succeeded in baptizing an emperor, but
according to *Emperor of China*, by the late seventeenth century
they claimed 16,000 converts in Beijing.

Kangxi commissioned a string of garden palaces, including
in the Fragrant Hills in the west and on Jade Spring Mountain.

Some were built on the foundations of Jin pleasances or Ming villas. The Yuanmingyuan (Garden of Perfect Brightness) to the city's northwest was his gift to his fourth son and heir, the Yongzheng emperor. Yongzheng (*r.* 1722–35) adored the Yuanmingyuan, adding audience halls so that he could administer the empire from there.

It was Yongzheng who, faced with southern courtiers who spoke impenetrable dialects such as Cantonese and Fujianese, decreed a unified system of pronunciation for *guanhua* ('official language', or Mandarin) based on the Beijing dialect; Manchu was called *guoyu* – the 'language of the state'. (Two centuries later, a Qing scholar proposed a 'common language', *putonghua*, also based on the Beijing dialect, for the people at large; in the 1950s, the Communists adopted the name *putonghua* for the national language. On Taiwan they call it *guoyu*.)

As emperor, Yongzheng virtually abandoned the Forbidden City. Like many others of the Qing's ruling Aisin Gioro clan, he found it claustrophobic. (Barmé's *Forbidden City* quotes a later Qing emperor describing the palace as a warren of 'dank ditches with vermilion walls and green-tiled roofs'.) The *wangfu* that had been Yongzheng's childhood residence became a detached palace he called Yonghe Gong (Palace of Eternal Harmony). After Yongzheng died in 1735, his son and successor, Qianlong (*r.* 1736–95), ordered the Yonghe Gong's turquoise roof tiles replaced with imperial yellow and, in 1744, transformed it into a temple. Known as the Lama Temple in English, it's still called by its palace name in Chinese.

Through a combination of military conquest and religious diplomacy, Qianlong brought Tibet and Xinjiang under Qing rule and expanded China to its current size. His reign was famous as one of the country's most prosperous ages. Master carpenters, weavers, wine-makers, coppersmiths, chandlers and their guilds and products further enlivened the *hutong* of the Outer City. Many famous *lao zihao* (old brands) of Beijing, such as Tongrentang pharmacies and Quanjude Peking Duck restaurants, hark back to those days. The Outer City grew even more famous for its entertainments following an official ban on restaurants, theatres and brothels in the Inner City from 1671. Among the patrons of the Dashila'r wine shops in the 1670s was the old rake, tippler, opera librettist and literary genius Li Yu, the author of the erotic novel *Rouputuan* (*Mat of Flesh*), who got about town with a lively entourage of pretty and clever young things.

The people of Qing Beijing were mad for opera. When four great troupes arrived in Beijing from the provinces in 1790 to perform at the palace for Qianlong's 80th birthday celebrations, Peking Opera – a distillation of poetry, dance, music, aesthetics, humour and philosophy – was born in the mix. Among the theatres Qianlong built inside his palaces for the entertainment of himself and his court was the three-storey Pavilion of Delightful Melodies, which featured trapdoors and other mechanical devices that allowed actors to appear and disappear as if by magic and fly like immortals across the stage.

Qianlong was a connoisseur, collector and patron of all the arts. He amassed an almost incomprehensibly large collection of artistic treasures from around the empire. Learning that Khubilai Khan's famous black jade wine vessel had ended up in a Daoist temple as a pickling jar, he purchased it for 1,000 pieces of gold and installed it in Beihai's fortress-like Tuancheng (Circular City), where it is on display today. Qianlong also rebuilt the Temple of Heaven's iconic Hall of Prayers for Good Harvests, expanding the round building to its current size and retiling the roof a uniform cobalt blue. More Buddhist temples were built in two decades of Qianlong's reign, in Beijing and elsewhere, than in the entire Ming dynasty.

Qianlong greatly enlarged the Yuanmingyuan. Carrying on with work begun in Yongzheng's time, landscape designers and architects recreated in its gardens scenes from famous Chinese poems and paintings through the sculpting of hills and valleys, lakes and islands as well as the artful placement of temples and pavilions. Among the Yuanmingyuan's follies was a 'Shopping Street', modelled after a market in southern Suzhou. There, the emperor and his consorts bargained for silks and other goods from eunuchs who played touts and merchants, while other eunuchs acted the parts of pickpockets.

PEKING OPERA

Drawing inspiration from Chinese history, literature and philosophy, Peking Opera is considered the very essence, *jingcui*, of Chinese culture and civilization. A range of archetypal characters from flirtatious young women to mighty generals (pictured), ferocious villains, brave heroes, wily ministers and clever servants strut its stage. Actors train for a lifetime to master the demanding combination of vocal performance, stylized movement and martial arts that the art form requires.

During Peking Opera's golden age, the late Qing and early Republican periods, it was wildly popular in common teahouses and princely mansions alike. Mao's wife Jiang Qing recreated the form as the Revolutionary Model Opera, introducing exotic elements such as ballet and orchestral music and replacing Confucian morality tales with revolutionary ones. The best of these, such as *Taking Tiger Mountain by Strategy*, were propagandistic but stirring and engaging entertainment.

The end of the Cultural Revolution saw a revival of traditional Peking Opera. Yet as China moved into the modern era, the opera's slow-paced, back-circling narratives and elliptical language has largely failed to engage younger generations. Today the government vigorously promotes it in schools and in the media (Chinese Central Television has a dedicated opera channel), but its audiences are ageing and dwindling.

Within the Peking Opera world itself, debate rages about the possibilities of and limitations on innovation. Pander to popular tastes and the form may change beyond recognition; stick to tradition and it risks becoming a museum piece. The rote, pallid performances in tourist-oriented shows demonstrate how bad Peking Opera can get when it loses its connection with its audience. Yet at venues like Beijing's Mei Lanfang and Capital theatres, a virtuosic performance can still stir a packed house of aficionados to thunderous applause and a chorus of bravos ('*Hao!*') that recall the opera's glory days.

Peking Opera 'Painted Face' general.

Original copperplate engraving of the Jesuit-designed Palace of the Calm Sea.

If caught, the thieves were caned; if successful, applauded. In the lakes, the emperor boarded miniature junks fitted with brass cannons to play naval games with his eunuchs.

Qianlong commissioned the Jesuits Jean Denis Attiret, Michel Benoist and Giuseppe Castiglione to design European-style buildings and water features for the gardens as well. They created grand, mock-Rococo buildings of stone and marble, furnished with calligraphy and Gobelins tapestries, carved jade and Venetian glass. Mechanical fish and birds cavorted in a marvellous fountain and the magnificent bronze heads of the twelve Chinese zodiac animals spat plumes of water to mark the hours.

The first British ambassador to the Qing court, Lord Macartney, declared the beauty of the Yuanmingyuan beyond description. Macartney had come to persuade Qianlong to trade with Britain; the British craved Chinese tea and porcelain. Qianlong didn't see the point of trade: 'We possess all things', he responded. Believing that the expensive magnifying glass that Macartney gave him was a magical talisman by which England might conquer China, the emperor ordered it destroyed. Hammers couldn't break it, so eunuchs buried it on the palace grounds in a (sadly unmarked) grave.

In honour of his mother's 60th birthday, Qianlong built another pleasure palace on the site of a nearby Jin pleasance, where the Mongols had created their reservoir. Completed in 1764, the new palace, overlooking Kunming Lake, was named Qingyiyuan (Garden of Clear Waves).

When Qianlong retired, it was to the northeast corner of the Forbidden City, where he built a miniature of the Forbidden City itself, filled with art and with dedicated spaces for study, contemplation and entertainment. Despite the dazzling accomplishments of his reign, by its end a dangerous gap had opened up between rich and poor, even in Beijing, and within the Banners themselves. On just one February night during the first year of the reign of Qianlong's son and successor Jiaqing (*r.* 1796–1820), several thousand homeless – mostly refugees from natural disasters – froze to death in the capital.

Nothing captured the sense of a waning civilization more than Cao Xueqin's masterpiece *Hong Lou Meng* (*Dream of the*

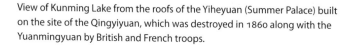

View of Kunming Lake from the roofs of the Yiheyuan (Summer Palace) built on the site of the Qingyiyuan, which was destroyed in 1860 along with the Yuanmingyuan by British and French troops.

Red Chamber, also titled *The Story of the Stone* in translation). Originally distributed in handwritten copies at temple fairs, it is considered the greatest Chinese novel ever written – and a uniquely comprehensive record of the customs, language, culture and mores of Beijing at the height of the Qing.

By the nineteenth century Britain had discovered there was one thing they could sell into China, albeit illegally: Indian opium. Aided by the French, the British literally blasted their way into the Chinese market with gunships in the Opium Wars of 1842 and 1858, forcing the Qing to cede control over Chinese ports including at Shanghai and Tianjin.

In 1860 the British commander of the Second Opium War, James Bruce, 8th Earl of Elgin (and son of 'Marbles' Elgin), dispatched a delegation of over 30 British and French subjects to Beijing to demand even more punishing concessions. Qing officials imprisoned the emissaries in the Yuanmingyuan and bound, beat, caged and tortured them. Half died.

As 17,000 British and French troops marched towards Beijing from Tianjin, the Xianfeng emperor (*r.* 1850–61), Qianlong's grandson, fled with his court to a hunting palace in Chengde, hundreds of kilometres away. The French proposed flattening Beijing and the Forbidden City in retribution. Elgin preferred to inflict a symbolic wound. They would burn down the emperor's beloved Yuanmingyuan. Only a small handful of eunuch guardsmen remained to guard the most beautiful garden palace the world has ever known. Their chief threw himself into Fuhai (Lake of Good Fortune) in despair. After an orgy of looting, in which the foreigners' southern Chinese camp followers enthusiastically participated, the soldiers set fire to the buildings. They also plundered and burned other imperial pleasances including the Qingyiyuan. For two days Beijing glowed saturnine with flames and cinders rained over the city. Many of the Yuanmingyuan's exquisite wooden Chinese buildings disappeared in the inferno, leaving only the now emblematic collapsed columns and stonework of the Jesuit piles.

Local Chinese souvenired whatever survived; palace treasures began popping up for sale in the antique shops at Liulichang. Abroad, masterpieces from the Yuanmingyuan were exhibited

TV crew filming at the ruins of the Yuanmingyuan.

at the Tuileries in Paris and at the Crystal Palace and British Museum in London. Some went under the hammer at Sotheby's. A regimental captain presented Queen Victoria with a Pekinese from the garden: 'Lootie'.

The shame-ridden Xianfeng emperor died in Chengde in 1861, at 30 years of age. Victor Hugo condemned the sacking: 'We Europeans are the civilized ones, and for us the Chinese are the barbarians. This is what civilization has done to barbarism.' A participating British captain characterized it as 'wretchedly demoralising work for an army'. But Elgin always insisted it was an act of 'justice', not 'vengeance'. In the Chinese collective consciousness, the burning of the Yuanmingyuan remains a powerful and emotive symbol of Western imperialist arrogance towards China.

Another 'unequal treaty' forced the Qing to allow foreign ambassadors the right of residence in Beijing. A Legation Quarter sprang up at the old Yuan dynasty rice markets,

Dongjiangmixiang (East Glutinous Rice Lane), which became Dongjiaominxiang (East Mingling of Peoples Lane). The Americans occupied a former hostelry for representatives of vassal states, the French acquired a decaying mansion with a magnificent garden, and the British leased a house belonging to the imperial clansman Prince Chun, sending the annual rent in silver ingots by mule cart every Chinese New Year. The Chinese Imperial Customs Service, headed by the Irishman Robert Hart from 1864, moved into Jinyu (Goldfish) Hutong.

Xianfeng's son, the six-year-old Tongzhi emperor (*r.* 1861–75), took the throne under the supervision of his mother, Empress Dowager Cixi and her co-regent, Xianfeng's official empress and Cixi's cousin, Ci'an. Inspector-General Hart, who had unique access to the court, observed that by his early teens Tongzhi appeared 'to be living awful fast. Women, girls, men and boys – as fast as he could, one after the other.' By nineteen, Tongzhi was dead, officially of smallpox, though some whispered it was syphilis.

Tongzhi, whose short reign had overseen a partial reconstruction of the Yuanmingyuan, left no heir. Cixi manoeuvred her three-year-old nephew on to the throne as the Guangxu emperor (*r.* 1875–1908) and continued her regency. A forceful, complex and controversial personality, Cixi dominated the politics of the late Qing, ruling from 'behind the screen', at first together with Ci'an, for nearly half a century.

In the 1880s, a 'self-strengthening' movement drawing on Western technology saw Beijing linked by telegraph cables with Tianjin and Shanghai. In 1888, intrigued by railways, Cixi had tracks laid for a miniature train pulled by eunuchs to take her from her quarters in the Lake Palaces to the Studio of the Quiet Heart on the north shore of Beihai where she liked to take lunch. It would be 1896 before Beijing got its first proper railway line, a link to Tianjin.

Guangxu turned sixteen in 1887, but Cixi held on to power. When a blaze destroyed several palace structures in 1888 and lightning struck the Temple of Heaven in 1889, burning down its sacred circular hall, Cixi's critics called the disasters signs of Heaven's displeasure.

The court decided to rebuild the Qingyiyuan as the Yiheyuan (Garden of Cultivated Harmony, or Summer Palace) in the hope Cixi would retire there and leave the emperor to rule. Because wars, natural disasters and rebellions had strained the treasury, the court diverted monies from the Board of Admiralty to fund the project, while ordering builders to harvest stones, bricks and tiles from the Yuanmingyuan, dismantling the Tongzhi era reconstructions.

On summer evenings Cixi's ladies-in-waiting rowed into the Summer Palace's Kunming Lake to insert parcels of tea into the hearts of lotus flowers; they retrieved them, infused with scent, in the morning. In winter, Bannermen skated on the lake in formations for her amusement. In 1860, foreign soldiers had vandalized a marble boat Qianlong had built in Kunming Lake; Cixi had it rebuilt with modern touches such as paddlewheels. She also had a special theatre constructed for her beloved Peking Opera. Amply diverted, Cixi left her nephew to rule.

In 1894–5, following a disastrous naval war with Japan, China was forced to sign yet another punishing treaty. Word that navy funds had been diverted to refurbish Cixi's marble pleasure boat created a scandal. A group of loyal but forward-looking intellectuals persuaded the 24-year-old emperor to enact political, economic and military reforms along the lines of those that had transformed Japan into a modern power. On 11 June 1898, Guangxu launched the reforms. Wary of sabotage by his aunt and her conservative, eunuch-dominated

Cixi's Marble Boat at the Yiheyuan.

The Summer Palace, a pictorial map from 1888.

cabal, he asked a young military commander with a reputation for progressive thinking, Yuan Shikai, to help restrain Cixi. Yuan turned informer. Under Cixi's orders, he detained the emperor instead.

Cixi confined Guangxu to a pavilion on Yingtai (Ocean Terrace), an island in the Lake Palaces, where he would pass almost all the rest of his days. On 28 September, imperial guards escorted six of the leading reformists out of the Inner City gate of Xuanwumen to the execution ground at Caishikou (Vegetable Markets). They were beheaded in front of 10,000 spectators on a site occupied today by a Walmart. Cixi assumed the power of regent once more.

Corruption spread. Infrastructure decayed. Relief funds failed to reach victims of natural disasters. A new peasant movement arose seeking to protect court and country from the foreign menace. The Society of the Righteous and Harmonious Fist – known in English as the Boxers – practised martial arts rituals they believed made them impervious to swords and bullets. After cutting a murderous swathe through isolated missionary communities in the provinces, they began trickling into Beijing in early 1900, conspicuous in red headbands and girdles. Some citizens welcomed the Boxers and even joined them. The Boxers had a strong ally at court in the person of the powerful Prince Duan.

China was now a country of 350 million people, of whom nearly 700,000 lived in Beijing. Less than 900 of Beijing's residents were foreigners, most of whom lived in the Legation Quarter, which now included churches, tennis courts and so many other amenities that the British diplomat Clive Bigham remarked that one could pass the summer there 'and never leave the precincts of civilisation'.

On 8 June the Boxers cut railway tracks and damaged electricity lines in the southern suburbs. They set fire to the Peking Racecourse, primarily patronized by foreigners, just south of the city. Days later, they marched in force through the city gates, saluted by imperial guards. Xenophobic to a fault, the Boxers attacked Chinese shops selling 'Western goods' such as paraffin lamps. They destroyed rickshaws, a recent import from Japan. As tensions rose, the violent-tempered German envoy, Baron Clemens von Ketteler, beat and murdered a young Chinese boy. On 20 June imperial troops allied with the Boxers shot the baron dead. They also killed a Japanese envoy, Sugiyama Akira, cutting out his heart.

The Boxers burned down Dong Tang (the Eastern Cathedral, built in the late nineteenth century on the site of Johann Adam Schall von Bell's house), killing a French priest and untold numbers of Chinese Catholics. Ten thousand Boxers laid siege to Bei Tang (the Northern Cathedral) in which over 3,000 converts were sheltering, attacking it with flaming arrows and explosives. Tens of thousands of Boxers and sympathetic imperial troops laid siege to the Legations, where thousands more Chinese Christians were now also sheltering. During the 55-day siege, nearly 3,000 missiles landed inside the legations; 76 people were killed and 179 were wounded. Among the injured was the correspondent for *The Times* of London, the Australian G. E. Morrison, shot in the buttocks. The besieged survived on the diplomats' stores of champagne, the flesh of their horses and donkeys – and rice, flour, watermelon and wine sent round, surreally, by Cixi.

Outside China, the story positions Westerners at the centre of the action – Hollywood's *55 Days at Peking* (1963) even starred Flora Robson as Cixi, dispensing Oriental inscrutabilities such as 'The voice of the nightingale is still; I hear only the sound of crows' as Robert Helpmann knelt at her feet, screwing up his eyes to play a scheming Prince Duan. But the Boxers inflicted the most pain on their own compatriots, torturing and killing tens of thousands of Chinese Christians. Their fires destroyed more than 4,000 Chinese shops, temples and homes in Dashila'r alone. An attack on the British Legation sparked a fire that burned down the neighbouring Hanlin Library, repository of China's most precious and irreplaceable historical manuscripts. Geremie Barmé has written how the Boxers also destroyed the last remaining structure in the Yuanmingyuan, the Porcelain Pavilion. Official Chinese accounts tend to skip over these facts; like Hollywood, the Communists prefer to keep the story simple.

Allied troops entering the city through an opening in the city wall.

On 14 August a motley force of some 17,000 British, American, French, Japanese, German, Russian, Italian and Austro-Hungarian troops, the Eight-Nation Alliance, arrived from Tianjin at the city walls. Japanese artillery pounded the city gate of Chaoyangmen into rubble. The Americans, entering through a breach in the walls, fired on Tiananmen itself. The following day, Cixi, her captive nephew and the court fled the city disguised as peasants.

The Allied forces killed many thousands of imperial troops and Boxers. They also looted the Forbidden City, the imperial treasury and the abandoned mansions of the nobility, and laid waste to Cixi's Summer Palace and another Qing pleasance on Jade Spring Mountain. Dividing the city into occupation zones, they indulged in an orgy of rape, beatings and murder before the Japanese enforced some semblance of order. Among those killed was the father of one of Beijing's most beloved authors, Lao She, who has written how a foreign soldier even stabbed his family dog to death. The soldiers destroyed imperial archives, including uniquely detailed, intimate records of palace life.

Foreign residents joined in the plunder. Morrison helped himself to what he considered a modest compensation of

Ninth U.S. Infantry in the court of the Forbidden City.

treasure from the Forbidden City, noting that Britain's Sir Claude and Lady MacDonald took away no less than 185 crates of loot. The British stole the imperial ancestral tablets from the Temple of Heaven for the British Museum and Germans carted off the massive, Jesuit-forged astronomical instruments of the city wall's Observatory Tower (returning them after the First World War).

Several months after the Allied troops departed, in September 1901, Cixi returned on a train decorated in imperial yellow silk. Beijing began, once more, to rebuild. The foreigners built a train station at Qianmen, convenient to the expanded, fortified and now exclusively foreign Legation Quarter. Like the foreign concessions in Shanghai, the Legation Quarter no longer recognized Chinese legal jurisdiction. New embassies were built in

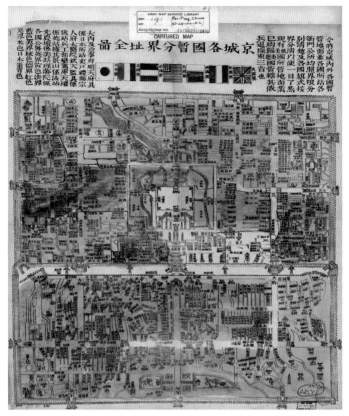

Map showing the occupation zones, 1900. According to the Chinese text, red represents German-controlled territory, blue for French, yellow for Britain, green or mustard for America and sky blue for Japan, and so on – but this only represents one period of the occupation.

national styles – mock-Gothic, mock-Baroque, mock-Empire; what the American writer and scholar George N. Kates describes in *The Years That Were Fat: Peking, 1933–1940* as 'a most oddly assorted juxtaposition of architectural *tranches de gâteau*'. Bullet holes still pocked the quarter's walls. In her intimate portrait of the city, *Peking*, long-time resident Juliet Bredon claims that 'at least one garden has Boxers buried under the lawns.'

Its former Chinese residents swelled the population of Dashila'r, also busily rebuilding. Artisanal workshops enjoyed boom times as foreign and Chinese alike replaced possessions lost in the violence. Foreign merchants opened shops selling imported goods on Wangfujing; the multi-storey Hotel de Pékin, at Wangfujing's southern corner, violated a centuries-old ban on buildings overlooking the palace walls.

In mid-November 1908, Cixi and the Guangxu emperor (who was never reinstated to power) died within a day of each other; she is believed to have poisoned him. The new, three-year-old Xuantong emperor (whose Manchu name was Aisin Gioro Puyi) bawled throughout his coronation. Three years later a republican revolution broke out in the south; the child-emperor abdicated and China's last imperial dynasty came to an end.

5 The Republic, Japanese Occupation and Civil War (1912–1949)

The reformist thinker Liang Qichao, who escaped execution in 1898 by fleeing to Japan, considered Beijing 'the hotbed of all evils'. In his view, as quoted (and translated) in Geremie Barmé's *The Forbidden City*,

> Not only has the land lost its pleasing features and the water its sweet taste but a thousand crimes, a myriad of scandals, and all the weird carbuncles and chronic diseases of this sinful world are concentrated there. If the political centre stays in Beijing, China will never see a day of clean government.

The southerners who led the revolution shared the sentiment, removing the capital of the new Republic of China to Nanjing. They left the dethroned child-emperor, now simply known as Puyi, free to occupy the residential sector of the Forbidden City with his rump court, even granting him a modest pension.

As the empire receded, Puyi was left, as Peter Quennell writes in *A Superficial Journey Through Tokyo and Peking*, 'the sole surviving coral insect of an enormous reef'. For nearly eight centuries that reef, the court, had been Beijing's chief employer and the driver of its economy. Its demise left nearly six in ten men in this city of over 700,000 unemployed.

Both the dispossessed and the revolutionary took out their anger and frustration on Manchus; some even lobbed home-made bombs over the walls of the princely mansions. Jittery Manchu Bannermen adopted Chinese surnames and dress. Many sold off their heirlooms and fled to the nearby cities of Tianjin or Qingdao. The turmoil unsettled the silk merchants

The 3-year-old Puyi with his father, Prince Chun, and younger brother Pujie.

of Qianmen, who carted their wares to the well-guarded Legation Quarter for safe storage. The shortage of silk on the market meant few in Beijing had new clothes for Chinese New Year. As a result of all these things, Chinese sources record that the 1912 celebrations were the most subdued in memory.

The military man who once arrested an emperor, Yuan Shikai, had helped the Republican government persuade the Qing court to retire. His price was the presidency. When he also demanded that the capital return to Beijing, a government delegation travelled north to dissuade him. The silk merchants had just reopened for business when soldiers rampaged through the city, looting, murdering, setting fires and damaging the city's new telephone exchange. The terrified envoys took refuge in the Legation Quarter. Yuan made his point: without him in charge up north, anything could happen. Especially if he wanted it to.

In April the Republican government transferred to the dust-blown north with as little enthusiasm as had the Ming court of Yongle. A wary parliament set up in the city's southwest, and government agencies, schools and enterprises found quarters in former princely mansions. Yuan established his offices in the Lake Palaces of Zhongnanhai, building himself a two-storey villa and furnishing it à la Louis XIV. (*The Forbidden City* describes Yuan arriving at a winter meeting with foreign diplomats on a red and gold sled pulled by servants in frock-coats and top hats, a leopard-skin rug over his lap.) He carved out a new gate, Xinhuamen (New China Gate), in the walls of the Imperial Precinct, on the site of the Qianlong era Tower for Delighting in the Moon, for the entrance to Zhongnanhai.

Members of Puyi's 'little court' filed into the north gate of the Forbidden City daily, changing into ceremonial garb once inside. The southern, or 'business' half of the palace began its transformation into a museum to safeguard the collections of all the city's palaces – treasures from which were already appearing in antique shops at Liulichang and overseas. The arrangement also kept the throne halls off-limits to Puyi and any restoration-minded regents.

No one was sure if the Republic would hold. In Beijing, more men kept the Manchu queue than elsewhere in China. Yet with no more imperial regulations on how people should dress, people experimented: both Manchu and Chinese women in Beijing adopted high-collared, narrow-sleeved, side-fastened dresses inspired by the traditional Manchu man's gown. As Antonia Finnane writes in *Changing Clothes in China*, the vogue for *qipao* (Banner robes) spread to Shanghai, where cosmopolitan Shanghainese tailors transformed them into the body-hugging frock also known by the Cantonese name *cheongsam* (long shirt). Even Puyi played dress-up in a Republican general's uniform until his guardians forced him back into his dragon robes, caning the eunuchs responsible.

For the first time since 1648, Han Chinese were legally allowed to live in the Inner City, even if in practice they had been quietly returning from the mid-nineteenth century onwards. Theatres, hotels and restaurants could also set up inside the walls. The Western District soon rivalled Dashila'r for commerce and entertainment. Peking Opera was in its heyday; rickshaws whisked its greatest star, Mei Lanfang, a male player of female roles, from performance to performance.

In 1914 Beijing got its first modern administration, a municipal council. The council smoothed and paved the pot-holed streets, nicknamed 'incense burners' after their thick accumulation of dust. It tackled the problem of the malodorous open sewers, some of which originated in kiln pits where the bricks for the Ming Outer City wall had been fired.

According to Barmé, the council used ornamental rocks, stelae and bricks from the Yuanmingyuan to transform both the imperial Ancestral Temple and the Altar to the God of Land and Grain in the former Imperial Precinct into Peace Park and Central Park respectively. Central Park's playgrounds, restaurants, bowling alleys, teahouses and photography studios drew families, prostitutes, students and wealthy burghers alike. Yet as Juliet Bredon wrote in *Peking*, at the time, old folk grumbled about the sacrilege, saying that if people wanted somewhere to hang out, they should visit a temple.

In 1916 the Australian G. E. Morrison, who'd lived in Beijing since 1897 and served for a time as Yuan Shikai's adviser, observed:

> Peking you simply would not be able to recognise except by its monuments. Macadamised roads, electric light, great open spaces, museums, modern buildings of all kinds . . . motor cars (there are I think at least 200), motor cycles more numerous than we care for, and bicycles literally by the thousand. New roads are being driven through the city in many directions and the Imperial city wall is now pierced in a dozen places.

Yuan had determined that a railway line should ring the outside of the city wall. The construction dismantled enceintes and sluice gates, and left arrow towers literally on the wrong side of the track. Feng shui masters fretted that the railway strangled the city, and warned that each new breach in the walls caused the city to leak *wangqi*, imperial spirit.

Yuan was keen on *wangqi*. In 1914 he'd donned imperial robes to conduct rites for the winter solstice at the Temple of Heaven. The following year he dissolved parliament, declaring himself emperor 'by popular demand'. After his death in 1916, parliament reconvened but a power struggle erupted. The president asked a provincial military governor, Zhang Xun, to help quell a rebellion by the premier. Unwittingly, he repeated the Ming general Wu Sangui's mistake: Zhang, a Qing loyalist who still wore the queue, arrived in the summer of 1917, put down the rebellion, and placed Puyi, now eleven, back on the throne with himself as regent.

The Republican government sent a warplane over the Forbidden City. The emperor and his courtiers dove under tables as a missile exploded at the Gate of Honouring the Ancestors, wounding a sedan-chair carrier. A second bomb fell in a palace lake. A third landed near a cluster of terrified eunuchs but, as Puyi recounted in his 1964 memoir *From Emperor to Citizen*, failed to explode. After a twelve-day reign, Puyi abdicated a second time; Zhang Xun, the 'Pig-tailed General', took refuge in the Dutch Legation.

China slid into the violent chaos known as the Warlord Era. For the next twelve years, rogue generals and their troops took turns fighting over, occupying, plundering and abandoning parts of China including Beijing. As Lao She wrote in his novel *Rickshaw Boy* (1936), war became as much a part of the cycle of Beijing life as 'the sprouting of spring wheat'. One of Beijing's more rapacious occupiers dynamited and looted the tombs of Qianlong and Cixi, leaving their stripped and mutilated corpses out to rot.

In 1898 Peking University had replaced the imperial college of Guozijian. By the Warlord Era it was China's largest, most prestigious and progressive centre for higher learning. Cai Yuanpei, its president from 1917, recruited some of the greatest cultural figures of the era to teach there, including the writer and satirist Lu Xun, the philosopher and *Dream of the Red Chamber*

The May Fourth Demonstrations as represented by a frieze at the base of the Monument to the People's Heroes in Tiananmen Square.

scholar Hu Shi and the radical publisher Chen Duxiu. (Chen later co-founded the Chinese Communist Party with the university librarian Li Dazhao, whose assistant in 1918–19 was a young Hunanese called Mao Zedong.)

In 1919 the Treaty of Versailles that ended the First World War ratified Japanese claims over former German concessions in Shandong province. On 4 May 1919, furious at the ongoing insults to Chinese sovereignty, 3,000 students marched from Peking University to Tiananmen and thence the Legation Quarter. Sympathetic townspeople swelled their ranks. Mass arrests sparked more protests, strikes and boycotts of Japanese goods. The May Fourth Movement that began in Beijing galvanized the nation and sparked a cultural renaissance.

Progressive intellectuals argued that Confucianism, with its innate conservatism and hierarchical thinking, dragged China backwards. In editorial offices and presses around Liulichang, they published books and journals that promoted vernacular literature, science, democracy and women's rights as vital to national salvation. Despite the conservatism of his 'little court', even the former emperor Puyi was exposed to Western learning from 1919 in the form of a new tutor, Reginald Fleming Johnston, whose Mandarin he found easier to understand

Liulichang Street: from imperial brick kiln to the centre of literary ferment.

than that of some of his southern courtiers, even if, as he admitted in *From Emperor to Citizen*, the Englishman's blue eyes made him 'uneasy'. Puyi took the English name of Henry and to the horror of his minions, cut off his queue in 1922, the same year that the Imperial Precinct lake Beihai was turned into a public park.

With China in chaos, the court's pension dried up. Suspicious of the extent to which his eunuchs were plundering imperial treasure, Puyi ordered an inventory. On 27 June 1923 a mysterious fire consumed the Palace of Established Happiness, repository of 6,643 priceless objects. Diplomats partying on the roof of what is today the Raffles Beijing Hotel saw the flames; the Italians dispatched a fire brigade to help put it out. Only 387 items were recovered; the missing included 2,685 gold Buddhas and 435 porcelain, jade and bronze artefacts. Puyi ejected nearly all remaining eunuchs (over 1,500) from the palace; as Barmé notes in *The Forbidden City*, many promptly opened antique shops around Qianmen. On 5 November 1924, another warlord turfed Puyi himself from the palace. Puyi moved into the Japanese embassy with his own plunder, 1,000 or so imperial artworks and artefacts, before decamping to Tianjin.

For all the decades of energetic looting, the Forbidden City was still home to more than a million antiquities. On

10 October 1925 the inner courts of the Forbidden City opened to the general public for the first time as the Palace Museum. Among the museum's most popular exhibitions was the Clock Pavilion, showcasing the Western novelty clocks once wound by Jesuits.

Missionaries established Yenching (a variant spelling of the old city name of Yanjing) University on the ruins of imperial gardens in the city's northwest, giving the Chinese language a new word: *xiaoyuan*, literally 'school garden', meaning campus. The Yuanmingyuan yielded more stones and bricks for the university's buildings, but by then the pickings were slim. Following the collapse of the Qing, the Yuanmingyuan's caretakers had even sold its trees and wooden bridges for charcoal.

A similar fate threatened Beijing's city walls. The American architect E. N. Bacon called them 'man's greatest single architectural achievement on the face of the Earth'. Lao She wrote poetically of the tiger-eye date trees and golden chrysanthemums growing along their solid, tranquil base, and the ducks that paddled the surrounding moat. But wherever they crumbled, unsentimental residents pilfered bricks. Made desperate by a collapsing economy, officials joined them, selling bricks to pay government wages.

Rickshaw Beijing: City, People and Politics in the 1920s by David Strand and Madeleine Yue Dong's *Republican Beijing* are two excellent English-language sources that document, among other things, the increasing desperation and impoverishment of Beijing in that era. According to Strand, in January 1926 soup kitchens in Beijing fed 30,000 people daily; in March, 80,000. That spring alone, 250,000 refugees from warlord-ravaged areas nearby entered the city. One out of four people in Beijing were poor or destitute; many others had clothes and enough to eat, but precious little else. A Chinese researcher of that era quoted by Strand discovered rickshaw puller households 'so poor that the family slept without bedding on dirt floors in rooms emptied of possessions except for a pile of pawnshop tickets'.

At the start of the Republican period, 90 per cent of Beijing's buildings were *siheyuan*, courtyard homes. As the population swelled, many of these were converted into multi-family tenements called *dazayuan*. With up to 60 people living in homes designed for one family, mansions degenerated into slums.

Warlords continued to fight over the city. Warplanes belonging to the 'Mukden Tiger', Zhang Zuolin, another Qing loyalist, dropped bombs on the city including near the Temple of Heaven, killing an elderly woman. Demobbed soldiers, many still armed, contributed to rising disorder and crime. Bankers, foreign diplomats and merchants banded together to pay the salaries of police and militia.

In this seething, distressed city, about 60,000 people, including erstwhile public servants, craftsmen, shopkeepers, musicians and even the odd Qing general and Manchu nobleman took up the punishing yoke of the rickshaw puller. In *Rickshaw Beijing*, Strand describes how a flat terrain, widespread poverty and the desire to display status on the part of those who still had money made rickshaws central to Beijing life. A uniquely Beijing literary genre of 'rickshaw literature' came into being, Lao She's *Luotuo Xiangzi* (*Rickshaw Boy*, also translated as *Camel Xiangzi*) its most famous example. 'The rickshaw', Strand writes, 'seemed to carry with it a natural air of melodrama that poets, professors and editorialists found irresistible.'

Streetcars came to Beijing in 1925. For the first time, Beijing people could easily work and play outside their immediate neighbourhoods. Streetcars also delivered people to the entertainment district at their terminus: Tianqiao (Heaven's Bridge), a 2.6-sq.-km hook of land in the Outer City north-northwest of the Temple of Heaven. Formerly a passageway for the procession of the emperor, the 'Son of Heaven', to the Temple of Heaven, the area was once a favourite idyll of scholar-officials. Daoist priests sold medicinal herbs by the bridge, antique sellers followed. In the sixteenth century, when the southern suburbs were walled, Tianqiao was the thriving marketplace at the heart of the Outer City. The following century, the shops, restaurants and theatres exiled by the Qing from the Inner City flooded into the area.

By the twentieth century, crowded, down-at-heel Tianqiao was famous for the rich, disordered bargains of its markets and the marvels of its entertainments, including storytellers, wrestlers, 'cross-talk' comedians, a man who performed stunts on a donkey's back and, according to accounts quoted by Madeleine Yue Dong, a snake swallower who could make serpents emerge from his ears. It was there, in 1912, that women performed opera in public for the first time. With *hutong* named Yanzhi (Rouge) and Pitiao (Pimp), Tianqiao was also notorious as a hive of criminal activity, with hundreds of brothels and opium dens. It too inspired a unique Beijing genre of fiction. Tianqiao had its dark shadow in the Badlands east of the Legation Quarter, described by Paul French in *Midnight in Peking* as 'the playground of the foreign

Rickshaws waiting for custom at the Qianmen Railway Station.

Pomegranates and persimmons in a *siheyuan*.

COURTYARD LIVING

Traditional Beijing life revolved around the *siheyuan*, or courtyard house, and its grander cousin the *wangfu*, or princely mansion. Both were structured around rectangular courtyards so perfectly aligned with the points of the compass that their residents could tell the hour by the movements of the shadows. Some were humble, and some were grand.

The great Beijing writer Lao She wrote of both types in his novel *Beneath the Red Banner*. The narrator recalls how in winter, 'the wind found its way into our home from every conceivable direction.' He lies on the *kang*, the brick sleeping platform with a built-in stove common to dwellings across northern China, and grows itchy with the combined warmth of the sun's rays and the heat from the tin stove inside the *kang*. He then thinks about the homes of the officials and the rich, which have brass or iron stoves, potted plants and lovely curios decorating the *kang*. He thinks about how in the grander homes, in cages hung under the eaves, song-birds stretch their wings and sing while servants prepare 'Mongolian gazelles and Manchurian pheasants' for the coming New Year's feast. His family, he says, loves plants too, but 'we couldn't afford plum blossoms or narcissuses'. Instead they have two 'gnarled' date trees, 'one behind the screen wall which stood behind the front gate of our house, the other by the foot of the southern wall'.

Courtyard homes are still notoriously difficult to heat, their upkeep can be expensive and plumbing remains an ongoing challenge. Yet given the large-scale destruction of the old city and the division of so many remaining courtyard homes into multi-family tenements, even a humble courtyard home is today considered a treasure by anyone lucky enough to own or occupy one.

underworld', another infamous site of brothels, opium dens and a criminal hang-out.

In 1926 the right-wing authoritarian Chiang Kai-shek, who had led the Nationalist Party following Sun Yat-sen's death in 1925, launched the Northern Expedition to mop up the warlords, turning violently on his erstwhile Communist allies in the process. In June 1928 Chiang arrived at the gates of Beijing, seeing off the warlord *du jour*.

Chiang ordered trees planted outside Tiananmen to limit spaces available to protesters. In *Republican Beijing*, Madeleine Yue Dong describes how Chiang primly renamed a number of *hutong*: Choushuikeng (Stinky Pond) became Cuihuawan (Emerald Flower Creek), Gouyiba (Dog's Tail) became Gaoyibo (Upstanding Old Man) and Jizhua (Chicken Feet) became Jizhao (Propitious Sign) Hutong. Han names replaced Manchu and Mongol ones; Uighur Village in the Haidian area became Weigongcun (Gentleman Wei Village). As for Beijing, it became Beiping (Northern Peace) – Chiang moved the capital back to Nanjing. The diplomats, comfortable in the Legation Quarter, were reluctant to follow; the Americans kept their embassy in the north.

Workshops in the Qianmen area continued to produce *cloisonné*, painted lanterns and carved lacquerware. Yet as late as the 1930s, this city of 1.5 million had scant modern industry aside from some factories producing matches, glassware and government uniforms. Beiping, as Dong shows, was forced to rely on other parts of China and foreign imports for almost everything else, including foodstuffs and medical supplies.

In 1929 the city's rickshaw pullers petitioned and eventually rioted against the streetcars that, alongside inflation, had bitten painfully into their livelihood. It was the worst public disturbance since Yuan's troops ran amok in 1912.

A more deadly threat lay north of the Great Wall. In 1931 the Japanese invaded the Manchurian homelands of the northeast and one year later established the puppet state of Manchukuo (Manchu Nation) with Puyi as emperor. In Beiping itself, the Japanese maintained a shadowy presence, controlling the black market and running opium dens.

In 1933 Chiang Kai-shek secreted more than 600,000 palace treasures out of the palace ('about one tenth of the entire imperial patrimony', according to *The Forbidden City*), shipping them to Nanjing. (They now reside in Taiwan's Palace Museum.) Dong writes in *Republican Beijing* of how residents feared that this indicated that the Nationalists were unwilling or unable to defend the city from Japanese attack.

Despite the turmoil, as historian John K. Fairbank has written, the period between 1901 and 1937 was a 'rare and happy time for foreigners in Peking'. Those with money shopped in the modern department stores and speciality shops of Wangfujing – called Morrison Street in English after the Australian correspondent – and in the antique shops that the visiting English poet Osbert Sitwell described as grander than those of Rome or Venice. They bought Italian wines, shopped at a French grocer, socialized at a Swiss hotel, had their hair done by white Russians and their clothes made by British tailors. In summer they rented temples in the Western Hills, or swam in a new public pool at the Lake Palaces, relaxing later, perhaps, on a former imperial barge in Beihai over a banquet cooked by one of Cixi's erstwhile chefs.

For the less well-heeled there was the colourful area just east of the Legation Quarter, adjacent to the Badlands and inhabited, in Fairbank's words, by

> remittance men of alcoholic dignity, sociable widows of diplomatic background, superannuated musicians, stranded poets fond of boys, budding art collectors, sincere scholars, patriarchal ex-missionaries, archaeologist-priests, a whole Maughamesque cast of characters . . . entranced by the sights, sounds, cuisine, and service of Peking.

Pierre Loti, who pronounced the city the last refuge on earth of the unknown and marvellous, Victor Segalen, George N. Kates, Osbert Sitwell and Harold Acton were among those writers captivated by the city, 'slipping', as the historian Susan Naquin puts it in *Peking: Temples and City Life*, 'into the luxurious calm of the (partially imaginary) life of a Chinese scholar'.

Sitwell's *Escape With Me!* (1939) is a classic foreign memoir from that time:

> the northern sun spatters both the moving people and the many static surfaces of paint with the flat, sparkling discs of a picture by Canaletto. Everyone is talking, laughing, shouting, buying or selling. Carts are rattling and jolting, and cattle are being driven through the best streets by swearing farmers' boys, armed with long sticks. A line of heavily laden, double-humped camels, proud but melancholy, are making a progress down the sandy track at the side of the broad road just beyond the Palace Walls.

The sense that a unique urban civilization was nearing extinction permeates George N. Kates's exquisite *The Years that were Fat* and informed guidebooks like L. C. Arlington and William Lewisohn's *In Search of Old Peking* (1935). A visit to the ancient capital where everywhere, 'roofs sag and pillars crumble', wrote Peter Quennell in his delightful *A Superficial Journey*, was 'a dream of desolation and declining splendour'. Segalen in particular regretted all attempts to modernize or renew the city.

Lu Xun described foreigners who wanted old ways preserved because it made their travel more interesting as 'loathsome'. Lao She satirized them in the character Mr Goodrich in *Si shi tong tang* (*The Yellow Storm*).

The Forbidden City was litter-strewn. Other monuments were collapsing. The Badlands and Tianqiao festered with vice and even the monks of the Lama Temple had grown notorious for assaults and thievery. Yet, thanks in no small part to the writers mentioned above, the ancient capital's mystique in the West had never been more potent. In 1934 the government decided to develop Beiping as a tourist destination.

The Japanese were already enthusiastically publishing guidebooks and picture books about the city, ominously conceptualizing it, as Naquin points out, within an expanded Japanese empire. On 9 December 1935 students in Beiping marched en masse to demand that Chiang's government fight the Japanese, not the Communists. Once again, the city's students provoked a national movement.

Beiping had grown to incorporate surrounding villages, including the small fortress-town of Wanping, built in the late Ming to defend the city from the rebel Li Zicheng. The Yuan dynasty Marco Polo Bridge crossed the Yongding River outside Wanping's west gate. On 8 July 1937 the Japanese instigated a military incident at Marco Polo Bridge. Their artillery pummelled Wanping, whose walls still display the scars of the first battle of Japan's full-scale invasion of China. In August, Japanese trucks and tanks rolled up Qianmen Street.

The Nationalists abandoned the city to spare it from attack. The Japanese declared Beiping the capital of the puppet provisional government of the Republic of China, calling it Beijing once more. Until 1940, when they massacred and raped some 300,000 people in Nanjing and moved the capital to that brutalized city, Beijing served as the command centre for Japanese forces in north China. The Japanese interned foreign residents and press-ganged Chinese citizens into slave labour, killing any who disobeyed orders and raping and murdering with impunity. They plundered the palaces and converted imperial gardens into farmland and fisheries to supply their forces, levelling hills in the Yuanmingyuan and filling in many of its lakes and streams. They imported huge quantities of drugs, licensing some 600 opium dens, mostly in Dashila'r; by 1942 one in seven residents in this miserable city, some 250,000 people, were addicts.

After Japan's surrender in 1945, the Nationalists took over the city once more, but as Beiping, retaining Nanjing as their capital. Corruption blossomed and inflation bloomed; a bag of flour soon cost Beijing residents 500,000 yuan. After civil war broke out between the Nationalists and the Communists in 1946, refugees swelled the population to 1.7 million. Air drops of rice and flour on to the ice of Beihai could not feed the starving city.

In January 1949 600,000 People's Liberation Army (PLA) soldiers surrounded the city – the last siege of a medieval walled city, as historian C. P. Fitzgerald has noted, in the twentieth century. From an airfield in the Dongdan Sports Ground, the Nationalists offered the city's intelligentsia and cultural elites evacuation to Taiwan. Few took up the offer. As the journalist-historian Dai Qing has observed, 'How could China's men of letters ever abandon this of all cities?' Instead, they helped the two sides to negotiate. On 31 January 1949 the Nationalist commander Fu Zuoyi surrendered and Beiping was 'peacefully liberated'.

In May the Communist newspaper *People's Daily* announced plans to 'build the people's New Beiping!' and convert 'the ancient feudalist city into a modern productive city'. The Communists sent army officers to speak with the influential architect and conservationist Liang Sicheng, son of Liang Qichao. Liang Sicheng loved the city's architecture as much as his father had hated its politics. He'd written of Beijing that it had 'so much power in general design; such scale in spatial

The People's Liberation Army 'peacefully liberates' Beijing.

layout' that it was 'second to none in the whole world!' The Communists asked Liang to help them identify and protect the architectural treasures of Beijing. Liang raved to his friends about how 'wonderful' the Communist Party was.

By September, close to national victory, the Communists renamed the city Beijing. Just before 3 p.m. on 1 October, the chairman of the Communist Party, the former Peking University assistant librarian Mao Zedong, climbed the 100 steps to the rostrum of Tiananmen and proclaimed the founding of the People's Republic of China.

Mao Zedong announcing the birth of the People's Republic of China, 1 October 1949.

6 Revolution (1949–1976)

The first Communist mayor of Beijing was the PLA general Ye Jianying. His adopted daughter, the journalist Dai Qing, has described how Ye organized

> a unity municipal government that included people from both the old and new regimes . . . transport and communications were soon restored, prices stabilised, and business went back to normal. After years of war, people could finally pursue their lives in peace . . . Beijing, with a red flag now fluttering in its skies, seemed to give concrete form to the ideals of a lifetime: national independence, an end to corruption in political life, a thriving economy and peace for the people.

Within one year of taking office, Ye's administration removed 94,000 tons of sewage and rubbish, some of Ming vintage, from Beijing's streets and *hutong* (which now numbered 1,330). Lao She celebrated this achievement in his play *Dragon Beard Ditch*, in which the new government brings joy to a Tianqiao neighbourhood by filling in a rank, open sewer. *Hutong* names got a fresh scrub as well: Shit Field (Fenchang) became Exert Orderliness (Fenzhang) and Stinking Skin (Choupi) became Long Life (Shoubi). Some were renamed to avoid confusion: when the Communists took power there were sixteen *hutong* called Shoulder Pole and eleven called Flower Blossom.

The new regime scoured the city of vice, closing mah jong parlours, opium dens and brothels. In Dashila'r, the writer Xiao Qian witnessed the roundup of prostitutes, pimps, madams and their servants. He writes in his memoir *Traveller Without a Map* (1988): 'the whole lot of them . . . chased into trucks in one smooth operation . . . as dextrously as a post office sorts letters'. Pimps and madams were sent to execution grounds or labour reform camps; prostitutes were 're-educated' to become nurses and actors. Soon, Tianqiao's wild days were but a memory.

Following a precedent set in the early days of the Republic, the Communists remodelled thousands of historic temples as factories, schools and government offices in the 1950s. The municipal security bureau took over the thirteenth-century Daoist Dongyue (Eastern Peak) Temple, home of the enforcer-gods of the underworld. Peace Park was reborn as the Beijing Municipal Workers Cultural Palace. The Eunuchs' Temple and cemetery at Babaoshan (Eight Treasure Mountain) in the city's west, also a cemetery and crematorium under the Republic and the Japanese, became the Beijing Revolutionaries' Cemetery. Xinhua News Agency moved into the Republican era parliament building and Beijing's Communist Party School set up on a campus that included Matteo Ricci's tomb. The new government established hospitals, a museum and housing on the grounds of the Temple of Heaven.

The government nationalized many of Beijing's *lao zihao*, 'famous old brands', including Quanjude, home of Peking duck, and Tongrentang (House of Benevolence) pharmacy, renaming the latter the Number Five Chinese Medicine Factory.

The Palace Museum's first exhibition following the Communist victory was of Nationalist and American war crimes. The newly purposeful city had no place for the 'little amusements' of Bannerman culture. It banned pets and urged people to divest themselves of 'useless objects' like Ming furniture, some of which went for firewood. Barmé writes in *The Forbidden City*:

The new Communist government . . . effectively declared war on old Beijing, deeming its lifestyle of leisure, culture and consumption to be the hallmarks of Manchu decadence, supine betrayal of the national interest and the source of China's humiliation.

People even dressed more soberly. In *Changing Clothes in China*, Antonia Finnane quotes the poet Ai Qing (father of the artist Ai Weiwei) grumbling: 'Look along a street, and all you can see is a great sheet of blue and black.'

Another Beijing tradition the Communists scrapped was that of idly consuming what the rest of the country produced. Soon after the establishment of the new government, municipal Party Secretary Peng Zhen told the architect Liang Sicheng that Chairman Mao had declared that in the future the view from the rostrum of Tiananmen would be that of a forest of chimneys. The Beijing writer Zha Jianying describes the scene in *China Pop*: 'Peng patted Liang on the shoulders: "Imagine that, Mr Liang!"' He did, she writes, and 'almost fainted'.

As Beijing's newly appointed chief urban planners, Liang and another overseas-educated architect, Chen Zhanxiang, urged the preservation of the Inner City together with its walls. That 'forest of chimneys' could grow elsewhere. The walls themselves could become an elevated people's park, its moats reserved for boating and fishing.

The Communists' Soviet advisers dismissed these ideas as 'petty bourgeois' and impractical. Raze the old city to the ground, they said. Create a central plaza like Red Square and rebuild around it. Chen and Liang argued that the Soviet plan would displace nearly 200,000 people, intensify pressure on infrastructure, worsen traffic congestion and destroy priceless heritage. Mao didn't care. When working in Peking University's library, he felt scorned by the city's intelligentsia as a thickly accented provincial. Their beloved imperial monuments were but feudal impediments to the fulfilment of his revolutionary vision. Despite mounting the rostrum at Tiananmen numerous times, Mao never once set foot inside the Forbidden City itself. In 1952 Chen and Liang's pleas were answered by the sound of sledgehammers. The demolition of the walls had begun.

The government also condemned Beijing's *pailou*. Free-standing arches of wood, stone and glazed tile, some dating back to the Ming, *pailou* spanned streets and bridges to

A Beijing *pailou*.

commemorate virtuous women and righteous men. While not unique to Beijing, the capital had more *pailou* than any other Chinese city. Chang'an Avenue lost its *pailou* when it was widened and lengthened to give the city a more politically resonant east–west axis. Liang's appeal to preserve a landmark twelfth-century temple with twin pagodas just west of the palace also fell on deaf ears; the fattened boulevard rolled straight over it.

Six thousand factories began production in greater Beijing, straining Beijing's water supply and belching toxic smog into once famously clear skies. Michael Meyer writes in *The Last Days of Old Beijing* that 14,000 smokestacks punctuated 'the skyline like exclamation points proclaiming the city as: The nation's largest petrochemical base! The leading producer of rubber products, plastic, and refrigerators!' Textile industries clustered in the area east of Jianguomen (today's CBD) and chemical industries to the south. To the north was the electronics district of Jiuxianqiao (Drunken Immortal Bridge). There, architects from East Germany designed a top-secret military-industrial complex, the largest in both Asia and the Communist world, in the style of the Bauhaus. Completed in 1957, it covered nearly 150,000 sq. m. Its 10,000 workers enjoyed on-site dance halls, night schools, dorms, and swimming pools and baths heated by water in the plant's cooling towers. Among its products were the command components in long-range guided missiles. Its factory zones were identified only by number: 798, for example.

Po-faced Soviet-style apartment blocks sprang up to accommodate workers recruited from all over China. The tenement *dazayuan* courtyards grew more crowded than ever. As in the Republican period, high officials and government bodies occupied the best of the old princely residences and courtyard homes. Kang Sheng, a cruel aesthete in charge of Mao's secret service, settled into the lovely Purple Bamboo Garden, today a hotel, and Long March veteran Chen Yi moved into the former residence of Cixi's chief eunuch Li Lianying. The Ministry of Public Security requisitioned the mansion said to have inspired the setting of *Dream of the Red Chamber*, Gong Wangfu (see p. 231). The central leadership moved into the Lake Palaces of Zhongnanhai, Mao ensconcing

The newly widened Eastern Chang'an Avenue.

himself by the Republican era swimming pool in Kangxi's Garden of Abundant Nourishment.

The Legation Quarter walls came down. As China's diplomatic ties largely followed Chiang Kai-shek to Taiwan, the municipal government took over Japan's old mission and converted the French and British embassies into state guesthouses, the Ministry of State Security later occupying the British Legation. The government awarded the Dalai Lama, with whom it was still friendly, the American mission and Burma and East Germany acquired the Belgian and German embassies. Soviet diplomats moved into a sprawling early Russian Church mission in the city's northeast; Soviet advisers moved into the custom-built Friendship Hotel in the old Uighur district of Weigongcun.

Peking University occupied the 'garden campus' of the former Christian university Yenching and absorbed its arts faculties. Tsinghua University took over Yenching's engineering department. Within a decade, Beijing went from eleven tertiary institutions to 52, more than any other city or even province in China, and including specialist schools of filmmaking, petroleum extraction and aeronautics. Its student population surpassed 100,000.

Wu Han, a Ming history enthusiast, was deputy mayor of Beijing in 1956. Curious to discover if the Wanli emperor had got his wish and been buried with his beloved Lady Zheng, he defied an ancient curse and opened Wanli's tomb. Lightning struck the excavators. The tomb spewed miasmic black mist. But the mystery was solved. Wanli had been condemned to a loveless eternity with his official empresses.

That year, the Communist Party invited the Chinese people to critique its first seven years in power: 'let a hundred flowers bloom'. Liang Sicheng was among those who spoke out, declaring that with each brick stripped from Beijing's walls, he felt like his own skin was being sliced off.

By 1957 Mao had heard enough. Under the supervision of Secretary-General Deng Xiaoping, the party labelled half a million mostly well-educated people 'Rightists', condemning them to labour reform camps and internal exile. Though forced to write a 'self-criticism', Liang was spared the gulag; not so his colleague Chen Zhanxiang, the poet Ai Qing, nor, incidentally, the archaeologists who excavated Wanli's tomb.

In 1958 Mao declared that China was ready for a Great Leap Forward to true communism. He ordered a quadrupling of industrial and agricultural output. Some 1,400 new factories began operation in Beijing's Inner City, smokestacks breaking through yet more temple roofs. Three 'Communist Mansions' were built to serve as urban communes where hundreds of families shared one kitchen.

Beijing's water supply couldn't meet the frenetic demands of industry. The government mobilized thousands of people to dig reservoirs. One near the Ming Tombs proved useless. Another, by the Great Walls at Miyun, was more successful (see p. 203).

To celebrate the tenth anniversary of the People's Republic on 1 October 1959, the party recruited 10,000 'volunteers', including students and teachers, to build ten major structures for the capital in ten months: the Great Hall of the People and Museum of Revolutionary History on Tiananmen Square, the Revolutionary Military Museum, the Beijing Railway Station, the Minorities Cultural Palace, Minorities Hotel, Workers' Stadium, Overseas Chinese Mansion, Agricultural Exhibition Center and the refashioning of the Jin dynasty 'detached palace' of Diaoyutai into a state guesthouse in the Soviet style.

One of Mao's 'ten great buildings': Beijing Railway Station.

The factories of 798 manufactured the electrical components and lighting fixtures for all ten Greats and the loudspeakers for an expanded Tiananmen Square. At 400,000 sq. m, Tiananmen Square was now the world's largest plaza, five times the size of Moscow's Red Square. In its centre rose the obelisk Monument to the People's Heroes. Grandstands winged Tiananmen, over which Mao's portrait became a

Tiananmen Square, the Monument to the People's Heroes and, behind it, the Great Hall of the People.

permanent fixture. 'It took Chinese emperors centuries to build their fabulous capital,' mourns the architectural scholar Xiao Hu, 'but only a decade for the Party to obliterate its excellence.'

At the end of 1959 Mao officially pardoned Puyi, the last emperor of the Qing, who had spent a decade in a labour reform camp for collaborating with the Japanese. Returning to Beijing for the first time in 35 years, Puyi became a gardener in Beijing's Botanical Gardens and an ornamental plant in the

flowerbed of communist propaganda. In his autobiography *From Emperor to Citizen,* written with Lao She's help, the one-time master of the Forbidden City called the voter's card he received in 1960 'the most valuable thing' he ever owned.

The economically catastrophic policies of the Great Leap Forward, a string of natural disasters and a rancorous split with the Soviet Union, which subsequently withdrew all aid, threw China into a three-year famine that would claim well over 30 million – possibly 40 million or more – lives. In June 1959 an article appeared in the *People's Daily* that recounted a story in which the upright Ming official Hai Rui tells the Jiajing emperor, 'You think that you alone are right, you refuse to accept criticism and your mistakes are many.' The following year the story appeared in *Beijing Literature and Art* in the form of a play, *Hai Rui Dismissed from Office.* The anonymous author of both was Deputy Mayor Wu Han.

Though famine hit Beijing later than other parts of China, by June 1960 its granaries held only seven days' supply for its 6.7 million people. Starving citizens stripped the bark from the city's trees. A coalition of alarmed party leaders including Deng Xiaoping forced Mao to dismantle many of the Great Leap Forward policies.

Mao, unrepentant, transformed Diaoyutai into the headquarters of a camarilla of extreme-left revolutionaries who included his wife Jiang Qing and 'closest-comrade-in-arms' Lin Biao. The Cultural Revolution began in 1966 with Mao's call for the people to attack his enemies in the leadership: 'Bombard the headquarters!' A group of students from the elite middle school attached to Tsinghua University met in late May at the Yuanmingyuan, vowing to protect Mao and the revolution, calling themselves Red Guards.

Affirming the youths' 'right to rebel', Mao urged them to attack the 'class enemies' and 'revisionists' among their teachers and school administrators. The Red Guard movement snowballed. Mao whipped up the ideological hysteria at eight Red Guard rallies held in Tiananmen Square between August and November 1966, each attended by 1 million people from around the country. Mao charged the Red Guards

Mao greeting Red Guards at a rally in Tiananmen: 'Bombard the Headquarters!'

with defending the revolution against bourgeois thinking, Soviet-style 'revisionism' and the enemies within.

Red Guards demanded that Beijing be called Hongjing (Red Capital) and that its traffic lights be rewired so that red signalled 'go'. Beijing remained Beijing and traffic continued to flow on green, but the city's streets and *hutong* were renamed yet again, until over 100 *hutong* had the word 'red' in their names – there was also Xue Maozhu (Study Mao's Collected Works) Hutong and Hui Zi (Destroy Capitalism) Hutong.

Red Guards committed their first murder in August, of a vice-principal, Bian Zhongyun, whom they beat to death. (In 2006 the independent film-maker Hu Jie made a documentary about her murder, *Though I Am Gone*; it is banned in China.) During what became known as 'Bloody August', Red Guards murdered or drove to suicide 2,000 people in Beijing and tortured, maimed and traumatized countless others. On 27 August alone, 228 people met violent deaths in the capital. On a wall near the palace, students wrote 'Long Live the Red Terror' in their teachers' blood.

Cultural Revolution 'struggle session': a volatile blend of violence and public humiliation.

Red Guards ransacked the home of the Peking Opera star Mei Lanfang (who died in 1961) and attacked his widow. One day, they assaulted and abused 29 famous scholars, opera stars and writers at the Pavilion of Exalted Literature at Guozijian, the old imperial college next to the Lama Temple. Among them was the 67-year-old author Lao She. The following day, Lao She's body was fished out of Taipinghu (Tranquillity Lake) near Shichahai. It is unclear whether his death was suicide or murder. Red Guards called Liang Sicheng a 'contemptible pile of dogshit'; he was so ill from tuberculosis that they had to prop him up to beat him.

FAREWELL MY HISTORY

In 1993 two films tackled the city's gnarly post-1949 history. Chen Kaige's *Farewell My Concubine* follows the fortunes of two Peking Opera actors from childhood in the 1930s through the Cultural Revolution. Banned and unbanned twice at home, it won the Palme d'Or at Cannes. Tian Zhuang-zhuang's *Blue Kite* tells the story of one ordinary Beijing family as it experiences successive political campaigns, from the Anti-Rightist Campaign of 1957 to the Cultural Revolution. *Blue Kite* also took prizes abroad. At home, not only was it banned, but Tian was told he'd never make a film again. (He has.)

Even the history museums only obliquely address the excesses and violence of the Maoist era, including the horrors of the three-year famine, as well as such events of the post-Mao era as what happened in 1989. Many of the Chinese-language works on Beijing history consulted for this book solved the problem of politically inconvenient history by concluding their narrative with 1949's 'liberation'.

If the official archives on the Maoist period in Beijing are guarded for now, there are plenty of historical sources available outside of China, including in Hong Kong. These include photographs, documents, memoirs and oral histories, as well as documentaries such as Hu Jie's *Though I am Gone*; *Morning Sun* (2003) by Boston's Long Bow Group, about the Cultural Revolution; and *The Gate of Heavenly Peace* (1995), on the events of 1989. Like Australian director Bruce Beresford's feature film of the ballet virtuoso-turned-defector Li Cunxin's memoir *Mao's Last Dancer* (2010), they circulate in bootleg editions in China, one of the only places in the world with a thriving black market for its own history.

A still from *Farewell My Concubine* features a young blond boy actor.

One morning that August, Nancy and David Milton, teachers at the Beijing Foreign Language Institute, noticed students walking with tins of petrol and 'the happily expectant air of summer picnickers', on their way to burn down the British embassy. The mob beat the diplomats fleeing the flames, and sexually assaulted the women, before People's Liberation Army soldiers whisked the Britons to safety.

The Workers Stadium hosted 10,000-strong 'struggle sessions' of prominent victims such as deputy mayor Wu Han, who died in 1969 after a brutal beating in prison. In *The City of Heavenly Tranquillity* Jasper Becker quotes Eric Gordon, a British journalist put under house arrest in the old city from 1967–9, as describing the constant 'roar' of the struggle sessions as 'like the moaning of a gigantic animal crouching over the city'.

Mao urged the youth to eradicate the Four Olds: old thinking, culture, customs and habits. According to Michael Meyer, of 6,843 catalogued relics in Beijing, '4,922 were smashed to dust, along with thirty of the eighty remaining historical sites.' Many people burned precious artworks and books in their personal collections rather than see them destroyed by Red Guards and be beaten for having them as well. Students and teachers furthered the Japanese project of planting crops in the Yuanmingyuan, filling in some of the remaining lakes to do so. Later a factory occupied the palace's last intact structure, the Zhengjue Temple.

The Red Guards didn't spare the dead, either. They vandalized the tombs of Matteo Ricci and Yelu Chucai, dug up the grave of the Jiajing emperor's cat Snow Brow on Jingshan and desecrated the Ming Tombs, attacking Wanli's corpse.

At the northern entrance to the Forbidden City, which had itself narrowly escaped being razed to the ground, Red Guards hung a sign reading 'Palace of Blood and Tears'. Installing a massive revolutionary sculpture called *The Rent Collection Courtyard* in the Hall for Worshipping Ancestors (the site of today's imperial clock exhibition), they forced the museum's scholarly deputy director, Shan Shiyuan, to stand next to it. As Barmé recounts, the thousands of daily visitors to the exhibition abused Shan, slapped and spat on him; a gang of provincial Red Guards beat him into near-total blindness.

Premier Zhou Enlai closed the Palace Museum to the public on 16 August 1966, two days before the first Red Guard rally at Tiananmen. When Red Guards from Tianjin tried to ram their way in with a truck, Zhou ordered in the army to protect it. The only leader with the authority and will to do so, Zhou also put Beihai Park, the Lama Temple, the Temple of Heaven and other key heritage sites in Beijing and elsewhere off-bounds to Red Guards.

The Red Guards eventually turned on one another. Between April and September 1967, rival factions fought hundreds of battles on Beijing's streets and campuses with weapons including machine guns obtained from backers in the army. According to Stephen G. Haw's *Beijing: A Concise History*, a single battle at Xidan in mid-August involved 3,000 armed combatants and hundreds of casualties. For 100 days, students, soldiers and workers fought at Tsinghua University with spears, guns, Molotov cocktails, grenades, slingshots, mines and even tanks; as William Hinton chillingly relates in *Hundred Day War*, 'corpses [lay] rotting in the cellar of the Science Building'.

By 1968 Mao's factional enemies were dead, imprisoned or silenced. He ordered the nation's youth to the countryside to 'learn from the peasants'. Many Beijing students ended up in Inner Mongolia or the bitterly cold 'Great Northern Wilderness' of the Manchu homelands. Surviving intellectuals and officials were dispatched to 'cadre schools' for re-education as well. The army under Lin Biao took charge, barracking in, among other places, the eighth-century Daoist Baiyunguan (White Cloud Temple).

Beijing once more became a front line. The threat was nuclear, and came from the Soviet 'revisionists'. In 1962, during a previous scare, the party mobilized the citizenry to dig underground shelters. In 1969 a second mass mobilization saw the people of Beijing, armed with picks and shovels, dig 85 sq. km of tunnels and shelters capable of holding 300,000 people 8–12 m below the surface. The underground city had drinking wells, schools, cinemas, military facilities and hospitals.

The old gate tower at Xizhimen, c. 1924: death by a thousand cuts.

Its construction swallowed up the last remaining bricks from the city walls and stones from the Yuanmingyuan.

By then, the only bits of Ming wall left were the gate and arrow towers of Qianmen, Deshengmen just west of the Drum and Bell Towers, the Ancient Observatory Tower at Jianguomen, the corner watchtower of Dongbianmen and Xizhimen in the western wall. As workers pulled down Xizhimen, Liang Sicheng observed the remains of a Yuan dynasty gate emerge from the rubble. Liang died in 1972, forced even on his deathbed to confess to political crimes.

In 1969 a shroud dropped over Tiananmen. Workers replaced termite-infested beams with wood from the old eastern gate of Dongzhimen. Kilns fired 10,000 new golden glazed tiles for the roof, replacing the imperial dragon motif with that of the sunflower, the symbol of the masses' devotion to Mao, their Great Red Sun. The rostrum was redecorated in the style of imperial audience halls.

The sinologist Pierre Ryckmans (pen name Simon Leys) lived in Beijing in the early 1970s as the Belgian cultural attaché. He writes in *Chinese Shadows* that 'Once, Peking managed the paradox of being a northern city with a [meridional] liveliness.' Now

the streets and markets have been shorn of their colours and spectacles; the noble city walls and gates have been pulled down; all the *pailou*s, which gave rhythm and graceful fancy to the streets, have disappeared . . . The jugglers, booksellers, storytellers, puppeteers, the thousands of craftsmen, the inns, the little shops and pubs, the antique dealers and calligraphy shops . . . in short, all that gave Peking its lovely, diverse, and wonderful face, all that made it into an incredibly *civilized* city, all that made the ordinary Pekingese – with their truculence, their verve, their quick and subtle mind, their art of living – a natural aristocracy within the nation, all this has gone, disappeared forever.

In 1971 Lin Biao died in a plane crash over Mongolia after he was discovered plotting to assassinate Mao. In February the following year, the American president Richard Nixon arrived in Beijing, his visit marking the first thaw in the Cold War. China's carefully calibrated welcome included no red carpet at Beijing's airport and the untranslated slogan, visible behind the honour guard, *Dadao meidiguozhuyi!*: 'Down with American Imperialism!'

Nixon met with Mao in the Lake Palaces. He toured the Forbidden City, bored and unaware of the frantic repair work that preceded his visit. He rode the new No. 1 subway line, ascending to the Chinese Military Museum by Beijing's only

Richard and Pat Nixon on the Great Wall in 1972: 'a great wall . . . built by a great people'.

escalator, and visited the Great Wall at Badaling, 'spontaneously' encountering high school students who'd been coached to receive him in a manner 'neither subservient nor arrogant'. He pronounced the ancient defences 'a great wall . . . built by a great people'.

That year, the People's Republic took the UN's China seat from Taiwan, and Japan and Australia resumed formal ties with Beijing. With more foreigners visiting or taking up residence in Beijing and even the Italian film-maker Michelangelo Antonioni in town, the government spruced up the main streets and calmed down some of the signage: Anti-Revisionism Hospital became Friendship Hospital and Anti-Imperialism Road in the old Legation Quarter reverted to its old name, Dongjiaominxiang.

One of the architects of the Great Hall of the People designed a new, seventeen-storey east wing for the two older buildings of the Peking Hotel. As the thirteenth storey was going up, it occurred to Zhou Enlai that Westerners staying there could spy on or even assassinate Chairman Mao from on high. Two storeys came off the blueprints. The fifteenth storey was quarantined for 'utilities' (allegedly including facilities for bugging guest rooms). A new 26.5-m-structure rose atop the Forbidden City's eastern wall to block sightlines into Zhongnanhai and, according to *The Forbidden City*, as an extra precaution, the windows on the hotel's western side were sealed shut.

Beijing's Xinhua Bookstore on Wangfujing offered up the first English-language textbooks in many years (Lesson one: 'Long live Chairman Mao!'). Beijing residents bought 600,000 in October 1972 alone. Queues formed too for the newly reprinted *Dream of the Red Chamber*. Soldiers returned to barracks, students to schools, cadres to offices. Jiang Wen's film *In the Heat of the Sun* (1994) captures the uncertain, restless mood of the capital in those revolutionary between-times.

Premier Zhou died on 8 January 1976. Tens of thousands of mourners lined the streets for the procession to Babaoshan. Qingming Jie, the traditional day for sweeping ancestral graves, fell on 4 April. People streamed on to Tiananmen Square, wearing white flowers of mourning and bearing

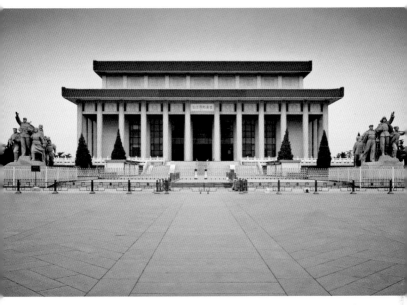

Chairman Mao Memorial Hall, the resting place of Tiananmen Square's sole legal occupant.

tributes of wreaths and poems dedicated to Zhou, which they lay at the steps of the Monument to the People's Heroes. Among these were scarcely veiled attacks on Jiang Qing and the Cultural Revolution: 'I weep while wolves and jackals laugh'. On 5 April, security forces moved in. There were beatings and arrests. The Party denounced the 'Tiananmen Incident' as a counter-revolutionary riot.

On 28 July a deadly earthquake ripped through nearby Tangshan. Beijing trembled. Frightened residents camped in the streets and Tiananmen Square. As when lightning struck the Forbidden City in the Ming, and the Temple of Heaven in the Qing, people whispered that the government had lost the Mandate of Heaven. Mao died on 9 September and, a month later, party leaders arrested Jiang Qing and her 'Gang of Four' cronies. Mao had wanted to be cremated. Instead, in 1977, his body was installed in a Lincoln Memorial-inspired Mausoleum on Tiananmen Square, in the centre of the historic north–south axis.

7 Reform: The First Decades (1976–2007)

Following Mao's death and the arrest of the Gang of Four in 1976, Beijing's 'sent-down' youth, 'Rightists' and other survivors of 30 years of Maoist purges and campaigns straggled back into the shabby, architecturally denuded city. Behind the walls of Zhongnanhai, party leaders engaged in a struggle over China's future direction. In the *hutong*, the people whispered and waited.

In October 1978 the Hunanese poet Huang Xiang arrived in the capital to paste an epic poem of lament and a lacerating critique of Mao on to a wall near Wangfujing. Thousands of people came to witness this extraordinary event. Then, in November, the party announced that the Tiananmen Incident of 1976 was not 'counter-revolutionary' but 'completely revolutionary'. These two events detonated an explosion of free political expression known as the Beijing Spring. At another patch of wall at Xidan, nicknamed 'Democracy Wall', tens of thousands of people posted or read poems, manifestos, demands for justice and expressions of hope.

Among them were a number of talented young Beijing men and women who would go on to play major roles in the culture of the post-Mao era. Some were associated with the samizdat literary journal *Today*, whose first issues appeared on Democracy Wall, and The Stars art collective (see p. 211). They included the poet Bei Dao ('Let me tell you, world, / I – do – not – believe!'), the future film-maker Chen Kaige (*Farewell My Concubine*), and the poet Ai Qing's son, the future artist-provocateur Ai Weiwei.

The popular ferment spread to other cities. It bolstered Deng Xiaoping's argument for economic reform, modernization and

Caricature of Jiang Qing on Democracy Wall.

an 'open door' to the outside world. Once he consolidated power, Deng shut down dissent. Huang Xiang and Wei Jingsheng, a Beijing Zoo electrician who had declared that the modernization China needed most was democracy, were among those arrested and imprisoned, Wei for a shocking fifteen years. By the end of 1979 Democracy Wall was no more.

In November 1980 Jiang Qing, now 66, and other surviving leaders of the Cultural Revolution went on trial at central police headquarters on Zhengyi (Justice) Road in the old Legation Quarter. Jiang was unrepentant: 'I was Chairman Mao's dog. I bit whoever he asked me to bite.' The court sentenced her to death, later commuting the sentence to life imprisonment (she hanged herself ten years later). In 1981 the party conceded that Mao had been wrong '30 per cent' of the time and 'rehabilitated' a number of his victims, including Ai Qing. It restored the posthumous reputations of Deputy Mayor Wu Han, the architect Liang Sicheng and the writer

Lao She, among others. The past dispensed with, the party ordered the people to *xiang qian kan*, 'look to the future', an incidental homophone for 'look to money'.

At the time, China's per capita GNP was one-fortieth that of the United States. Beijing may have been one of the best-off cities in China, but its hospitals lacked beds and kindergartens places. There were 1.3 phones per hundred people, many servicing whole neighbourhoods. The supply of electricity was unreliable, brownouts frequent. On clement nights people gathered at the base of streetlamps to study, chat or play cards. Even the public toilet blocks servicing the residents of the *hutong* since the 1960s had reached new lows of fetidness.

The city was now home to 9 million people. Living space had shrunk to an average of 3.5 sq. m per person; hardly big enough, as the journalist Tiziano Terzani observed in *Behind the Forbidden Door*, 'for a double bed'. Not that it was easy to buy a bed in those pre-consumerist times – Terzani noted that among the first signs of the new market economy was the sight of peasants carting homemade furniture into the city for sale from the back of their bicycle or donkey carts.

As the country slowly shifted from a command economy in which the state owned all the means of production and distribution to one that allowed for individual enterprise, other peasants brought fresh produce to what were called 'free markets'. The first individually and collectively run restaurants opened – and stayed open past the state diners' closing time of 6:30 p.m. When cloth rations ended in 1983, entrepreneurs set up silk and clothing stalls in narrow Xiushui Street in Jianguomenwai. Electronics shops opened at Zhongguancun, close by the universities of Haidian.

In 1979, the tallest buildings in the capital were the fifteen-storey Peking Hotel and the Soviet-style apartment blocks of the 1970s. The Peking Hotel boasted the city's sole café-cum-bar, but Chinese visitors had to show ID and be signed in. In 1982 the nation's first 'joint-venture' hotel opened at Jianguomenwai: the Jianguo. It had the foreign community in raptures at the then-singular delights of its French restaurant, café and bakery, and the ease of meeting Chinese friends there.

Yet even in 1983 Beijing could still impress with its bleakness. The Austrian photographer Inge Morath had lived through one war and documented the aftermath of others. Arriving in Beijing that year, she noted the ongoing food rations, general air of dilapidation and the darkness of the city at night, and remarked to her husband, the playwright Arthur Miller, that Beijing looked 'like a country after a great war'.

Beijing's foreign community was growing rapidly. By the end of 1984 about 500 foreign firms, including 70 banks, had established offices there. The 100-m-tall CITIC Building not far from the Jianguo would soon dominate the skyline in the city's east, while the revolving restaurant atop the brand new Xiyuan Hotel briefly became a source of wonder in the city's northwest.

The authorities scrambled to restore surviving heritage sites, even patching up the tomb of the Jesuit Matteo Ricci. But what to do with temples that Red Guard rampages had left without a single icon? Terzani relates how in a village outside Beijing, farmers had managed to protect the fine bronze Buddha of their local temple from the depredations of the iconoclasts, only to lose it to the Buddha-deprived Fayuan Temple. Such substitutions, largely undocumented, occurred throughout the capital.

Post-1949 history was an ideological minefield. Film-makers wanting to say something about it turned to the Qing, abusing the empress dowager Cixi as a handy, if facile stand-in for Jiang Qing. In 1986 the Italian director Bertolucci, meanwhile, filmed a fictionalized version of Puyi's life, *The Last Emperor*, shooting inside the Forbidden City with Peter O'Toole playing Reginald Johnston. But when the Beijing Film Studio went to make Lao She's *Rickshaw Boy* into a feature in 1983, the city had changed so much in just half a century that they had to reconstruct Old Beijing as a film set.

By 1984 traffic began to flow on the new Second Ring Road, which was laid on the foundations of the old Ming wall and above Line 2 of the Beijing subway (see pp. 195–9). Construction of a Third Ring Road and airport link got under way. The latter would replace the potholed, dusty and narrow

Bicycle traffic on Chang'an Avenue, mid-1980s.

airport road that was more like a street in some rural backwater, complete with donkey- and horse-cart traffic, than the approach to a world capital.

It was in 1984 too that six peasant families from Wenzhou prefecture in Zhejiang province defied the strict household registration system that dictated where people may live and work to settle in Nanyuan township, less than 6 km south of Tiananmen Square. Others from Wenzhou followed. These entrepreneurial southerners survived successive crackdowns on unauthorized internal migration to found a Beijing institution, 'Leather Jacket Village', ultimately supplying a range of goods to buyers throughout north China, the former Soviet Union and Eastern Europe.

In 1984 the party celebrated the 35th anniversary of the People's Republic in Tiananmen Square. Missiles and tanks demonstrated China's military might. Floats with giant robots,

Second Ring Road under 21st-century noon smog.

a wristwatch and an electric fan celebrated the consumer economy. A banner proclaimed: 'Time is Money'. A 1,000-piece band played and Peking University biology students contributed one unchoreographed note, raising a smuggled-in banner with a friendly hello to the country's leader: 'Xiaoping, *ni hao*!' (In a smaller, unnoticed security lapse, thanks to a pass slipped to me by a Chinese friend, I partied on the square that night with workers from Capital Steel.)

One April evening the following year, 15,000 people thronged the Workers Stadium for the nation's first-ever concert by a Western pop group: Wham! As George Michael belted out 'Wake Me Up Before You Go-Go', the crowds defied police orders to dance at their seats. The following year, China's first home-grown rock star, a trumpeter with the Beijing Philharmonic called Cui Jian, gave the country its own first rock anthem: 'Nothing to My Name':

Cui Jian.

I want to give you my hope
I want to make you free
But all you do is laugh at me, 'cause
I've got nothing to my name.

The Beijing Municipal Party Committee was outraged: 'How can one of our young people sing about having nothing when he has socialism?'

The writer Wang Shuo captured better than anyone else the freewheeling mood of Beijing in the 1980s. The descendant of Manchu Bannermen, Wang had been an army man, smuggler, pharmaceuticals salesman and the kept man of an airline hostess. He'd done time for snatching the cap off a policeman's head during the Tiananmen demonstrations of 1976. His novels, screenplays and short stories, including the one that was the basis for the film *In the Heat of the Sun*, were sharp, satirical and linguistically inventive portraits of Beijing's underworld and youth culture, and they inspired a new, enduring Beijing literary genre: '*pizi* (smartarse, hooligan) literature'. There was a time when everyone, from intellectuals to lift operators, seemed to be reading Wang Shuo (see pp. 148–9).

If the reforms offered opportunity to the entrepreneurial, in dismantling the old system of cradle-to-grave employment and welfare, they also contributed to a growing divide between haves and have-nots, and the rise of official corruption. Student protests erupted around the country, including in Beijing, in 1986–7. Deng Xiaoping blamed the popular, free-thinking university lecturer and astrophysicist Fang Lizhi for fomenting trouble; Hu Yaobang, the relatively liberal-minded Party Secretary-General, was also forced to resign.

In early 1989 Fang called on the party to release 'all political prisoners, and particularly Wei Jingsheng' in honour of the 70th anniversary of the May Fourth Movement and the 40th anniversary of the People's Republic. The poet Bei Dao and many other prominent intellectuals and cultural figures signed petitions in support. Together with the death of Hu Yaobang on 15 April, these ignited a student-led protest movement against corruption and for free speech and democracy. The protests eventually involved hundreds of thousands of people and culminated in the occupation of Tiananmen Square. Students camped on the square, made love on the square, and sang 'Nothing to My Name' on the square. The Tiananmen occupation was part Woodstock and part Berlin Wall, except when the wall fell in China, it fell on the people.

On 20 May the government declared martial law. People's Liberation Army (PLA) troops encircled the city. With students on a mass hunger strike, citizens flooded on to the streets in support, erecting, according to the *Beijing Evening News,* some 600 barricades along approach roads to the square. At 10 p.m. on 3 June, tanks and armoured personnel carriers rumbled towards the square, shooting unarmed citizens who stood in their way and crushing barricades, bicycles and even bodies under their treads. By 4 a.m. there were perhaps a thousand dead, including a handful of soldiers, and untold wounded. In *The Monkey and the Dragon* I've written in detail how the Taiwan singer-songwriter Hou Dejian and the future Nobel Peace Laureate Liu Xiaobo saved thousands of lives on the

overleaf: Pro-democracy demonstrations, 4 May 1989.

square itself by persuading the army to open a safe passage through which the students could retreat.

Later that morning, a Chinese Everyman gave the world the iconic image of those events when he stepped out into Chang'an Avenue to confront a line of tanks. To the movement's sympathizers, 'Tank Man' symbolizes individual courage in the face of state-sponsored terror. In official spin, he proves the army's restraint in the face of provocation. His identity and fate remain a mystery.

Following the suppression of what Mayor Chen Xitong labelled 'a counter-revolutionary rebellion' came a wave of arrests, interrogations and forced confessions. Aiming to deflect popular anger from the party towards – why not – nineteenth-century foreign imperialists, the government launched a nationwide 'patriotic education' campaign that included a slew of theatrical, film, television and literary works on the theme of the burning of the Yuanmingyuan.

On 11 January 1990 the government lifted martial law from Beijing in time to scrub up for the Asian Games later that year. Workers had already begun resurfacing Chang'an Avenue, where armoured personnel carriers and tanks had ground tracks into the bitumen. They replaced broken paving stones on Tiananmen, scrubbed away pro-democracy graffiti and patched the bullet holes in walls and buildings. Under tight security and the dumb gaze of the ubiquitous cartoon mascot Pan Pan the Panda, the Games went off without a hitch.

In 1992 some of the air shelter tunnel network opened to tourism and commerce. It would eventually house hostels, shops, bars, grain stores and even an ice rink. Other interesting underground developments were occurring in the cultural sphere. Wu Wenguang directed China's first independent documentary, *Bumming in Beijing: The Last Dreamers* (1990) about the city's artistic drifters. Rocker Cui Jian starred in a pioneering independent feature film, Zhang Yuan's *Beijing Bastards* (1993). In a lecture delivered at the China Film Museum in Beijing in March 2008, the film scholar Li Daoxin noted that never before *Beijing Bastards* had a post-1949 film dared to depict Tiananmen as shrouded in grey mist and

THE WORLD OF THE OPERATORS

There's a Beijing archetype called a *pizi*: a smartarse, a wiseacre, an operator full of schemes, some of which may be of dubious legality. A *pizi* is the sort of person you'd cross the *hutong* to avoid if they weren't so damn funny and perversely charming. The *pizi* may also have an element of another, older Beijing archetype, the *hutong chuanzi*, literally someone who circulates through the *hutong*, picking up and spreading news and gossip. And both the *pizi* and the *hutong chuanzi* owe something to the old Qing Bannerman culture of 'little amusements'.

Welcome to Wang Shuo's world. One of his most popular early works was *The Operators* (1987). In a memorable scene, an archetypal *pizi* called Yang Zhong approaches a woman waiting for someone on the street: 'Sorry, I'm late', he says. 'I rushed but still couldn't make it on time. Have you been waiting long?' Not for him, she tells him. 'Ah, but you were,' he says, 'you just didn't know it. No one else is coming.' He reveals he knows her name and that of the man she's waiting for:

> 'Wang Mingshui has a mole on either side of his nose.'
>
> 'The moles haven't gone anywhere. But early this morning he was called to attend an emergency, a leader was having a haemorrhage. So he called my company, and asked us to send someone to fill in. He didn't want to disappoint you. My name's Yang Zhong, I'm employed by the Three-T Company. This is my card.'
>
> 'Three-T Company?' Liu Meiping glanced suspiciously at the card Yang Zhong gave her. 'What's that? It sounds like some pest control service.'
>
> 'It's an abbreviation for *trust* us to solve your problems, *trust* us to relieve your boredom and *trust* us to take punishment on your behalf.'
>
> 'You're serious. What sort of people work there? People with no sense of shame and nothing else to do?'

The novella *The Operators* was one of Wang Shuo's most popular early works. In it, Wang Shuo captures the roguish humour, banter and verbal play that is an integral part of the Beijing vernacular, along with the

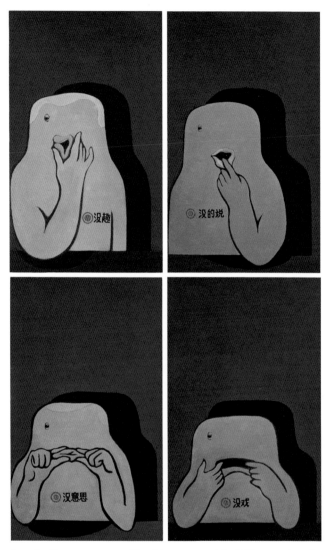

freewheeling entrepreneurship of the 1980s and the Beijing penchant for taking sly pokes at power – the incident described in the scene above appears to have been precipitated by a leader's problem with haemorrhoids.

Guan Wei, *4 Works: Without Interest, Nothing to Say, Not Interesting, Not Fun*, 1980, acrylic on canvas; the artist Guan Wei is also the decendant of darkness, as opposed to bathed in sunshine. Zhang's iconoclastic assault continued in 1997 with *East Palace, West Palace*, about the gay beat at the public toilets on either side of Tiananmen.

Four years before *East Palace, West Palace* screened at Cannes' Un Certain Regard, Chen Kaige's *Farewell My Concubine* became the first Chinese film to win the Palme d'Or. Set within the world of Peking Opera, the film climaxed with a searing portrait of Beijing during the Cultural Revolution.

By the time Chen shot *Farewell My Concubine* on the Old Beijing set built for *Rickshaw Boy*, what was left of old Beijing faced new threats from rampant development. In 1988 municipal and local governments were freed to raise revenue through the sale of usage rights to land. Many writers on Beijing and journalists including Michael Meyer, Jasper Becker, Philip Pan and the best-selling Chinese author Wang Jun (who introduced Liang Sicheng's story to a new generation of Chinese readers) have written eloquently of the destruction visited on Beijing's historic neighbourhoods as a result.

In 1993 the State Council belatedly set out limits for building density and height within the Second Ring Road. Yet Mayor Chen Xitong personally facilitated developments that broke State Council guidelines and even his own zoning laws. In 1995 he was charged with embezzling u.s.$2.2 billion and sentenced to sixteen years imprisonment (he was released for medical reasons in 2006). The citizens of Beijing hadn't forgotten his role in the massacre of 1989. Many covertly rejoiced at the news of his arrest just as their Yuan predecessors had when the tyrannous Ahema literally went under the hammer back in 1282.

By 1998, land rights sales provided the Beijing government with one-fifth of its revenue. According to Philip Pan, kickbacks, speculation and other forms of corruption put over $17 billion in the pockets of developers and local officials during the 1990s alone. Jasper Becker reveals in *City of Heavenly Tranquillity* how in Xuanwumen district, where nine out of ten original residents were ultimately forced out of their homes, a real estate company set up by the district government's Cultural Relics Bureau 'knocked down the listed properties [the Bureau] was supposed to be protecting'. There's a frequently-told joke, possibly originating with Wang Shuo, that the English word 'China' comes from *chai na* – 'demolish that'.

The men and women who are tearing down old Beijing and are builing the new, the 'foot soldiers of China's Industrial Revolution', as the journalist Jan Wong calls them in her book *Beijing Confidential*, are the migrant workers from the provinces. In the mid-1990s, Beijing's registered population reached 12.6 million; on top of that were 3 million 'illegals', more than the entire population of Beijing in 1949. For about 20 yuan a day (one-sixth the average Beijing wage at the time) these migrants, as Wong observes, did 'all the dangerous, dirty, exhausting jobs' that saw Beijing outstrip all other world capitals in the construction of tall buildings, roads and highways. They built two of the biggest train stations in the world, West Station, terminus for the express train from Hong Kong, and the enormous Beijing South Station, which, as the former China blogger for the *New Yorker* Evan Osnos has noted, consumed as much steel as went into New York's Empire State Building. Migrants mucked out the old public toilets and constructed the new ones for the 'toilet revolution' of 1996. It was they who uncovered the remains of Palaeolithic campfires while excavating the foundations of the Oriental Mall. Migrant workers also laid down the Third Ring Road and would eventually give Beijing a Fourth, Fifth and Sixth Ring Road as well as highways ribboning out in all directions, including to the Great Wall at Badaling in the north and Tianjin in the east. If one of them should get run over on the roads they'd built, however, their families could expect less than 80 per cent of the compensation due a legal resident – even their lives, Jan Wong points out, are 'literally cheaper'.

By 2002, according to the *China Heritage Quarterly*, about '40 per cent of the old city' had been 'levelled'. In 2004 the municipal government belatedly drafted regulations 'on the preservation of the Historical and Cultural City'. And yet, as the scholar Bruce Doar has written, official notions of heritage rarely include ordinary housing, which is only 'grudgingly' acknowledged in conservation planning. Between 1990 and 2007, according to the Geneva-based Center on Housing Rights and Evictions, 1.25 million Beijing residents were forced from

Migrant construction workers building Beijing.

their homes in the name of urban renewal. 'This is human upheaval', Thomas Campanella observed in *The Concrete Dragon: On China's 'Urban Revolution'*, 'on a scale seen previously only in time of war or extreme natural catastrophe.'

In 2003 Peking University hosted a conference titled 'Beijing: Urban Imagination and Cultural Memory'. Zha Jianying reports in *Tide Players* how Chen Danqing, an artist with an American passport, was the only participant to raise the protests and massacre of 1989. Chen argued that Beijing's 'urban imagination' had

> always been dominated by big power: emperors, Mao, and today's city authorities, real estate developers, and big international architects . . . And Beijing's cultural memory? Well it is full of holes or simply frozen.

He noted that all the other delegates confined their comments to events before 1949, when cultural memory is permitted to function. Zha says that, following a stunned silence, Chen received sustained applause.

In 2000 a Starbucks opened in the heart of the Forbidden City at the Gate of Heavenly Purity, where officials of the Qing had gathered for their dawn audience with the emperor. Along with McDonalds, KFC, Pizza Hut and other American fast-food chains, Starbucks had already metastasized throughout the city, but its presence in the palace itself struck many as a marble bridge too far. After a popular news anchor on national TV complained about the 'symbol of America's low-class food culture', half a million people petitioned to have the chain evicted. It packed up in 2007, replaced by the Forbidden City Café.

The architect Liang Sicheng's widow, his second wife Zhu Lin, as well as his (now deceased) son Liang Congjie and Lao She's son Shu Yi all became active in the battle to save what little is left of historical Beijing. Becker comments in *City of Heavenly Tranquillity* that the epic struggle for conservation has unfolded 'rather like in Lao She's 1953 play, *Tea House,* where in each successive act and each generation the same characters appear condemned to play the same roles'.

8 Ringing in the New

In 1954, having realized that the new government had no intention of listening to his pleas for the preservation of old Beijing, Liang Sicheng told Mayor Peng Zhen that in 50 years, he'd be vindicated by history. Almost on the dot of half a century, the city announced it would rebuild a section of the old city wall. It asked anyone still holding original Ming bricks to turn them in; 200,000 piled up in the collection centres.

The wall rose adjacent to the southeast corner watchtower of Dongbianmen (itself first renovated in 1981 and since 1991 home to the Red Gate Gallery – see pp. 213–14). As Liang had proposed, both the top of the wall and the grounds in the shade of its parapets were transformed into public parkland. According to statistics quoted in Michael Meyer's *The Last Days of Old Beijing*, 2,000 homes and 60 businesses that had sprung up on the site since the original wall's destruction fell before the demolition squads.

City planners also revived Liang and Chen Zhanxiang's concept of satellite towns as a way of lessening pressure on the city centre. The Millennial Monument west of Tiananmen (a grandiose replica of the marble sundial in front of the Forbidden City's main audience hall) sits on a second new north–south axis for the city, coincidentally right where Liang and Chen suggested locating the new government centre.

After Beijing won hosting rights to the 2008 Olympics in 2001, the city was thrust full tilt into preparations. Having pledged a 'Green Olympics' with no net growth in carbon emissions, the city poured over U.S.$12 billion into welcome environmental improvement. It expanded waste-water

Ming Dynasty City Wall Relics Park: what is old is new again.

treatment; served marching orders on a remaining 700 urban factories; planted tens of millions of new trees, including 83 km of 'greenbelt'; cleaned up 40 km of rivers and canals; and created new parks and gardens with fountains and artificial lakes largely fed by rivers of 'Category V' pollution levels (unfit even for irrigation).

The city also invested almost $73 million in conserving and renovating 100 heritage sites. Yongdingmen (Eternally Fixed Gate), the Outer City's largest gate tower before it was torn down in 1957, rose again in 2004. It was rebuilt on a smaller scale but to the greatest possible extent with traditional materials and techniques: workers applied tung oil to South African guaiacum columns with cow-tail brushes.

The restoration of Yongdingmen, first mooted in 1999, was part of a long-term plan to restore and extend the city's Ming era north–south axis. For the Asian Games in 1990, the city lengthened the axis at its northern end, from 7.8 km to 13 km; in the process it restored Wanning (Lasting Peace) Bridge by Shichahai. The Olympic Park would stretch the axis another 13 km northwards.

All of Beijing's UNESCO World Heritage Sites received a pre-Olympics spruce-up: sections of the Great Walls, Cixi's Summer Palace, the Temple of Heaven, the Ming and Qing imperial tombs, the site of Peking Man's discovery at Zhoukoudian and the Forbidden City (the restoration of which is due to be completed in 2020). Qianmen Street was done over as well, arguably in both senses of the phrase (see pp. 187–93).

Environmental and conservation improvements accounted for only part of Beijing's $44 billion facelift (ten times what Athens spent in 2004 and three times London's budget in 2012). The city built or upgraded dozens of sports facilities, including the architectural showpieces of the 'Bird's Nest' National Stadium and 'Water Cube' National Aquatics Center at the Olympic Green (see pp. 216–24). The Olympic Green is three times the size of New York's Central Park and features forest and lakes that allow it to serve as a much-needed 'green lung' for the city. The authorities also built an Olympic Village, now a complex of upscale apartments, and 250 new hotels.

Between 2001 and 2008 Beijing more than tripled the length of its subways to 200 km, with the goal of tripling that again and more by 2015. Beijing's fleet of public buses swelled to 20,000. Of these, 4,000 run on natural gas, more than in any other city in the world. Beijing Capital International Airport's dragon-shaped Terminal 3, which opened early in 2008, with an area of 986,000 sq. m (sixteen times the exhibition space of the Louvre), is the world's fifth-largest building in terms of floor space and can process 66 million passengers a year. It's hoped that, annually, 10 million of these will be international, Taiwan and Hong Kong tourists, which together with 200 million domestic visitors will allow Beijing to earn one-tenth of its GDP from tourism, ideally $10 billion a year.

On the stroke of midnight on New Year's Eve in 2008, the Bell Tower's 63-tonne copper bell, cast in the time of Yongle, rang out a propitious 108 times. The mercury had plunged to −10°C, but at an outdoor stage at the Millennial Monument, Hong Kong superstar Jackie Chan led several thousand specta-tors in singing the Olympics countdown song 'We are Ready'.

The Olympic Opening Ceremony was scheduled for the auspicious time of 8 minutes past 8 p.m. on the 8th day of the 8th month (a proximate homonym for 'Prosper! Prosper! Prosper! Prosper!'). As a giant digital countdown clock on Tiananmen Square ticked off the days, hours, minutes and seconds, preparations switched into high gear. Beijing cab drivers and neighbourhood committee members swotted up on English. The most blatant girly bars were closed down. The homeless and beggars were rounded up and shipped out for the duration along with the tens of thousands of migrant workers who'd built the Beijing of the Olympics but weren't required during it. Their makeshift housing, according to Lawrence Liauw's study of the 'Post-Olympic Urbanization of Beijing', was 'literally erased' as unsightly. (Those migrant workers who later returned – or arrived afresh – to carry on with the construction of the still-growing city would have to start again from scratch.) Security forces and neighbourhood committees kept a closer eye than usual on known 'trouble-makers'. Everyone was to smile. No one was to spit.

Beijing had promised clear skies and air that athletes could safely breathe. It delivered them via industry bans, cloud seeding by the Beijing Weather Modification Office and a strictly managed system of traffic management that kept half the cars off the road at any given time.

Beginning with the 29 fireworks footprints (digitally recreated for simultaneous television broadcast) that traipsed

'One World, One Dream', opening ceremony of the 2008 Beijing Olympics at the Bird's Nest Stadium.

across the sky from Yongdingmen due north to the Bird's
Nest and film director Zhang Yimou's grand-scale choreog-
raphy for the opening ceremony, through to the wealth of
gold medals mined by China's athletes, the Olympics was
widely hailed as a triumph for Beijing, its 'coming-out party'.
While prominent in international coverage, scandals such
as the revelation that the little girl who sang at the opening
ceremony was lip-synching for another deemed too unattract-
ive for the world's cameras, and concern about ongoing
human rights abuses, especially in Tibet, were ignored by
local media.

The following year, Beijing staged another spectacle, this
one to celebrate the 60th anniversary of the founding of the
People's Republic of China. Security was unprecedentedly
heavy, with police and paramilitary troops stationed throughout the centre of the city for days beforehand. Emerging from
the subway at Xidan, on my way to see the new propaganda
film *The Founding of a Republic*, I walked straight into the
machine-gun sights of a swat team ranged before a black
armoured vehicle; as I scurried off, every hair on the back
of my neck upstanding, I recalled dancing on the square in
the celebrations 25 years earlier. On the day itself, with the
exception of 30,000 invited guests, Beijing residents were
commanded to stay indoors and watch the celebrations on
television. If Beijing had 'come out', it was on its own terms.

Liu Xiaobo, the former lecturer at Beijing Normal University
who'd played a key role in the Tiananmen protests of 1989,
remained a leading and bold dissident voice. On Christmas
Day, 2009, he was sentenced to eleven years' imprisonment
for 'inciting subversion of state power'. In 2010, while still
imprisoned, he was named Nobel Peace Laureate.

In 2011 the Beijing artist Ai Weiwei was arrested while
leaving China on a legitimate passport and held for nearly three
months, eventually charged with evading taxes and kept under
house arrest. In 2012 his *Circle of Animals/Zodiac Heads*, a
recreation of the circle of bronze zodiac animal heads from
the Yuanmingyuan, was unveiled in New York in his absence.
While under house arrest, Ai Weiwei made a video of himself

and friends doing the Korean rapper Psy's 'Gangnam Style' pony dance, but with handcuffs, and uploaded it to YouTube.

It's hard to ascertain what most Beijing people know about these two men who have symbolized their city to the world in the second decade of the twenty-first century. Beijing residents born after the Mao era cannot easily access information about the Cultural Revolution, Anti-Rightist Campaign, Great Leap Forward or famine, much less the events of Democracy Wall or the 1989 protests. Not everyone is interested, either. Not since 1949 has a generation enjoyed such access to education, social freedoms, entertainments, travel and employment opportunities. The young people of Beijing today have almost too much with which to occupy themselves – forget Tiananmen Square.

The square itself is heavily policed and no longer open on all sides; fences funnel visitors through guarded underpasses. If a young Beijinger wanders from an exhibition on Bulgari or Louis Vuitton at the swanky new National Museum of China to the adjacent Revolution and History Museum on the east of Tiananmen Square, s/he will see only one photograph illustrating the decade of Cultural Revolution: the caption beneath ambiguously describes the period as a mistake that was manipulated by a 'counter-revolutionary clique' in a way that caused terrible suffering. On the worst famine in world history, the museum's text states: 'the project of constructing socialism suffered severe complications.' Li Zicheng, the murderous peasant rebel who overthrew the Ming, gets a glowing write-up, as do the Boxers. As I studied an exhibition case of Boxer weaponry, a woman approached with her young grandson. 'Do you know what the Boxers did with these?' she asked him. Gleefully, he cried: 'Killed the bad eggs!' With a sideways glance at me, as though curious if I understood, but not overly concerned, the grandmother responded, 'Correct.'

In an article published in 2006, the elderly historian Yuan Weishi pleaded for honesty in education on such subjects as the burning of the Yuanmingyuan and the Boxer Rebellion. By not facing up to the realities of the Boxers' extreme xenophobic violence, and by overlooking the torture and murder of the Western envoys by the Qing court that spurred Elgin's

The Galaxy SOHO shopping mall designed by architect Zaha Hadid.

actions, Yuan argued that the Chinese authorities were inflaming a dangerous breed of nationalism and irrationalism in foreign relations. The authorities closed down the journal that published Yuan's article.

Ideology, like history, is a work in progress in Beijing. For nearly a century, progressive intellectuals inside and out of the Communist Party have rejected Confucianism for its conservative social prescriptions. The Communist Party has become a fan, however, in recent years. On 11 January 2011 Beijing residents woke up to discover a 9.5-m-tall bronze statue of Confucius on Tiananmen Square in front of the National Museum. An online poll by the *People's Daily* found 62 per cent of the 820,000 respondents wanted him gone. In late April he was shunted to an internal museum courtyard. Beijing wags circulated text messages with jokes like the one claiming Confucius, a Shandong native, had been busted for not having a Beijing *hukou* (residence permit); a neo-Maoist website posted a photograph of the statue over which it superimposed the character *chai* – demolish.

One reason neo-Maoists have regained some traction in public debate (and why pro-democracy activism continues to ferment) is that although China has lifted itself from poverty, corruption and socio-economic inequality have reached levels that would make good King Zhao weep. The problem is not confined to Beijing, but because Beijing is where the most powerful people in China live and work, the abuses can appear all the more egregious: when a Ferrari crashes and kills someone in Beijing, chances are that the son of a prominent person is at the wheel.

The ultra-rich and ultra-connected in Beijing live in gated communities and do their shopping in Paris. The poor crowd the remaining *dazayuan* and wretched housing estates of the outer ring roads and fret over the rising price of vegetables. Between the two is a rising middle class that aspires to live in villa communities with names like Beijing Riviera or Merlin Champagne Town. Those in the upper spectrum may buy imported milk and organic vegetables at Jenny Lou's, a chain opened by an entrepreneurial peasant couple who once carted

Renovations in a *dazayuan* (tenement courtyard).

their vegetables into the city on the back of a flatbed bicycle.
Those in the lower spectrum don't lack for much, but still
take public transport. Which is not a bad idea – the 5 million
vehicles driven by Beijing's 20 million-plus residents keep the
city's roads in near-permanent gridlock. In August 2010 a
100-kilometre, 10-day traffic jam blocked up highways from
Beijing all the way to Inner Mongolia.

More than one in three Beijing residents today were born
elsewhere. The classic Beijing dialect, with its purring rhotic
vowels and distinctive vocabulary, is no longer the dominant
music of the street. Linguists note that today people speak
more quickly, in a higher pitch, with a lighter accent and
not as many 'silent' or dropped tones as in the past.

Close to 200,000 foreigners live, work and study in Beijing.
Over half are from South Korea. Just as Chinese immigrants
grew their Chinatowns abroad, Russians have their Russiatown

by Ritan Park, there are streets of Korean restaurants and grocery stores, and Sanlitun, inside the East Third Ring Road, is the site of Argentinian, French, Italian, Spanish and even Israeli restaurants and cafés, French hairdressers, international design shops, imported food shops, outlander bars and nightclubs, and even a Hooters.

The 1980s era clothing stalls of Xiushuijie have evolved into a multi-storey clothing bazaar. The guild-dominated *hutong* where, for example, you might find jade polishers or wok-makers, are no more, but there are massive shopping centres devoted to such specialized goods as electronics and eyeglasses. Most of the historical *hutong* have gone. In 2012, 600 were declared heritage-protected. Yet that year the photographer Xu Yong, who specializes in the subject of *hutong* photography, told the journalist Jaime Florcruz that, in his view, there were only 200 'honest-to-goodness' *hutong* left.

The old Inner City represents less than 1 per cent of Beijing's total area today. It has become a conurbation encompassing sixteen districts and two rural counties. At 16,808 sq. km, it's the size of Wales. In administrative terms, like Shanghai and other Chinese mega-cities, Beijing is a municipality with

Street scene, old 'Chinese city' south of Qianmen.

the status of a province. Its 440-km Sixth Ring Road, which girdles the city 15–20 km from the centre, cannot hold it. Nothing can contain its daily tsunami of rubbish, carted out to a mushrooming number of tips and mostly informal recycling centres that ring the city and are dubbed the 'Seventh Ring Road' by residents. This 'Great Wall of Rubbish' is the subject of independent film-maker Wang Jiulang's unnerving documentary *Beijing Besieged by Waste* (2011); the city continues to face serious environmental challenges.

As in the early twentieth century, the dust of demolition has raised clouds of nostalgia. 'Old Beijing' is new again. Publishers can't seem to produce enough books about Beijing history, customs, legends and personalities, including photography books and reproductions of old maps. Recent popular television series have included the 42-episode *One Hundred Years of Rongbaozhai*, set in a famous Liulichang antiques shop, and director Li Shaohong's 50-episode *Dream of the Red Chamber*. As *The Economist* observed in June 2012 of the fad for Qing drama in particular, 'It's a good time to be a Manchu on television'.

Today on the reconstructed Qianmen Street, you can enjoy your Republican era and eat Häagen-Dazs too. If the Lao She Teahouse west of Qianmen serves traditional Manchu snacks along with digestible bites of Peking Opera, the opera itself is in crisis, with thinning, elderly audiences and fierce internal debate over the limits of reform.

Cows graze on garbage in this still from the documentary *Beijing Besieged by Waste* (2011).

The Yuanmingyuan in bloom – and under reconstruction.

Controversies rage around the future of the Yuanmingyuan, as some advocate preserving the ruins as an eternal reminder of Western imperialist aggression and others argue for recreating its former glory (and better exploiting its tourist potential). The establishment of a winter amusement park with sledding and skiing and the development of theme parks and 'culture squares' on its periphery – and occasional shows in which valiant Chinese villagers shouting 'Kill the foreign devils!' fight stupid-acting dwarfs in woolly blonde wigs – have roused fury and despair among heritage scholars and conservators.

The conservationists and historians are fighting a difficult battle. With rising incomes across China and extended public holidays designed to stimulate travel and consumption, Beijing is inundated with domestic tourists. Long gone are the days when a visitor like Peter Quennell, who travelled to

Beijing in the 1930s, could wander in the palace for hours, 'unaccompanied', as he wrote in *A Superficial Journey*, 'save by the rhythm of your own footsteps'. On just one day in October 2012 alone, the Forbidden City hosted 180,000 visitors. The shoes of the tourists are wearing down the ancient paving stones and their exhalations are corroding the wooden buildings. Despite installing 1,600 alarms and 3,700 security cameras, the Palace Museum management struggles to combat theft, attempted theft and graffiti.

Other scandals have erupted in the Forbidden City over dubious conservation practices, termite infestation and even tax avoidance. In 2011, after a benefactor sponsored the meticulous reconstruction of the building consumed in the suspicious fire of 1923, the Jianfu (Established Happiness) Palace, public outrage forced authorities to scotch plans to convert it into an exclusive club for the über-wealthy and ultra-connected.

Beijing's past shadows and illuminates its present. In his 1930s memoir *Escape with Me!: An Oriental Sketchbook*, Osbert Sitwell made the observation, still true today,

> much of what Marco Polo writes concerning Cambaluc remains true of . . . modern Peking . . . the same vast population . . . the same great numbers of foreign merchants, travellers and provincial fortune seekers . . . [and its] air of luxury and cosmopolitanism.

The Line 10 subway station Jintaixizhao (Sunset on the Golden Tower), named for both King Zhao's tower, which once stood nearby, and the Ming dynasty painting commemorating it, is a reminder that Beijing has weathered many cycles of prosperity, corruption, decay and regeneration. Travel further north on Line 10 to where it hooks around to the west and it runs under the northern sector of the old Yuan dynasty city walls. The walls that once so impressed Marco Polo are now an uneven string of grassy knolls overlooking a revived moat in a Yuan Dynasty Relics Park that traverses seven city blocks. It is hard to imagine that

Tourists at the Meridian Gate of the Forbidden City.

this peaceful park, where lovers stroll and locals practice Tai Chi, overlooked by giant statues of Khubilai Khan and his court, was once the site of imperial grandeur, siege and desolation.

Lin Yutang, also writing in the 1930s, averred that, 'What are centuries elsewhere are but short moments in Beijing. Conquered many times, it has ever conquered its conquerors.' Yet the conquerors no longer come from outside China's borders. The architect Liang Sicheng's first wife, the great poet Lin Huiyin, whose work was admired by Rabindranath Tagore, had been as passionate a conservationist as Liang. She even threatened to kill herself at the city gates when the last of the walls came down, but died of tuberculosis first, in 1955. When Sitwell and Lin Yutang were writing about Beijing, she and Liang were living in a beautiful *siheyuan* courtyard house on Beizongbu Hutong in the East City, working on their collaborative landmark study of Chinese traditional architecture.

CHAI

The journalist and urban historian Wang Jun, author of a popular book on the architect-conservationist Liang Sicheng's efforts to save old Beijing in the 1950s, posted the following blog post on 10 July 2009:

> Although the Beijing Municipal Planning Authority has already ruled that there be no more demolitions of major buildings, that the old city is to be protected in its entirety, a notification of demolition was nonetheless posted on the walls of Bei Zongbu Hutong in the East City and the work of tearing down the historical home of the architect Liang Sicheng and his wife Lin Huiyin has begun.

In 1945, when the long war of resistance against Japanese invasion ended with Japan's surrender in the Second World War, Liang Sicheng publicly appealed for the victors to preserve Japan's ancient cities including Kyoto and Nara. Even as the Japanese were planning to erect a monument to him, Wang Jun notes, the wreckers in Beijing were flattening his house.

'Unless we have become completely alienated from our national culture, this is something no Chinese ought to tolerate.' Wang wonders if the developers knew that Liang and Lin helped design China's national emblem and the Monument to the People's Heroes in Tiananmen Square, or that the national prize for architecture is called the Liang Sicheng Prize. Regardless, they should at least know the 2004 and 2005 municipal and State Council laws forbidding further destruction of the old city. 'Chinese who love their country's traditional culture will pursue those who have trampled on our national cultural heritage until they have been forced by the law to take responsibility for their actions,' he promised, 'even if it takes several generations.'

Marked for demolition: the white-painted character *'chai'* condemns another *hutong* home.

Beizongbu Hutong is prime real estate by today's standards. Fuheng Realty, a subsidiary of the state-owned company China Resources, had their eye on it for some time. On the fourth day of the Chinese New Year holiday in 2012, when nearly everyone in China would be with family or on vacation, Fuheng sent their wreckers to pull down Liang Sicheng and Lin Huiyin's old home (see p. 168). Even the *China Daily* reported on the widespread outrage sparked by this particular demolition. The head of the Beijing Municipal Bureau of Cultural Heritage, Kong Fenzhi, told the state's Xinhua News Agency that it 'should never have happened'. Promising that the home would be rebuilt using traditional methods and materials, he contributed a phrase to the Chinese language, much parodied since: *weixiuxing chaichu*: 'maintenance-style demolition'.

Months earlier, authorities had conducted a poll to find the right words to describe the 'Beijing Spirit'. They announced that the winners were 'patriotism, innovation, inclusion and virtue'. Even as a propaganda exercise, it was lame, and Chinese netizens lampooned it with especial glee. Playfulness, wit and gentility were never going to make an official list but, although diluted by development, growth and globalization, neither have they disappeared. If Beijing has lost much of the lifestyle and physical beauty that earned it so many admirers in the past, it still retains something of its real spirit which, whatever happens, will live on in the vast and still growing body of literature, film and art that it has inspired over thousands of years.

THE CITY TODAY

Xiao Ju'er (Little Chrysanthemum) Hutong. In the several years since this photo was taken, the lane has filled up with shops, cafés and bars.

In the Shadow of the Drum Tower

As I drag my suitcase along Xiao Ju'er (Little Chrysanthemum) Hutong, I'm greeted with smiles and the simple welcome 'hui laile' – 'you're back'. The kids wave and call out 'Ayi', Auntie. I've returned to Beijing after a few months' absence to my favourite home-away-from-home, a small courtyard residence in a historic *hutong* belonging to a pair of Chinese sisters. Opening the handsome red door, the older sister greets me warmly, but with bad news: the night before, my bathroom ceiling fell down.

The false ceiling hangs at a 45-degree angle from one corner. I put down my bags and return to the *hutong*. Within five minutes, a neighbour has introduced me to a migrant worker from the provinces, Han: 'I trust him like my own son.' Han's crew is renovating the man's home inside one of the lane's warren-like *dazayuan*, divided courtyards.

The amiable Han follows me back inside, admiring the courtyard garden's pomegranate and persimmon trees. The dangling ceiling doesn't alarm him. By the following evening, he has replaced it for a total cost of $150 including materials. Even my host, who thinks I have the words 'I'm a Foreigner, Rip Me Off' tattooed on my forehead, is impressed. Han has done an immaculate job.

Unlike during the Qing dynasty or Republican period, you are unlikely to find travelling magicians, almanac pedlars or men with trained monkeys or bears trawling Beijing's *hutong* today. Itinerant snack vendors no longer carry sour-plum soup and almond tea in buckets dangling from the ends of shoulder poles. No one offers to light your lamps. But pedlars and tradesmen are still very much part of the life of the *hutong*.

As winter approaches, hawkers pedal flatbed bicycle carts through the *hutong* with stacked quilts; in spring, they're singing out their list of potted plants and flowers. They deliver briquettes of charcoal and take away old bottles and scrap. Vendors of the *Beijing Evening News*, a popular tabloid of local news, gossip and human-interest stories, announce their presence with a pre-recorded squawk from speakers attached to their bicycles.

If neighbours know who can do renovations, the neighbourhood committees – the party and state's eyes and ears on the *hutong* – know everything else. Chinese law requires non-citizens to register with the police within 24 hours of arrival. (Hotels register their guests automatically.) Once, I forgot. At the 25th hour, a small posse from Ju'er's neighbourhood committee knocked on the door to order me to the police station. Its other duties include seeing that everyone flies the flag on National Day and posting reminders to practise 'civilized behaviour'.

Civilization has a long history in this neighbourhood. Ju'er Hutong is one of sixteen *hutong* running east and west off the

Hutong flower pedlar.

Early morning traffic, Nanluoguxiang.

north–south axis of Nanluoguxiang (South Gong and Drum Street). Seven centuries ago, in the days of Khanbalik, the street was called Luoguoxiang, 'Arching Street', because it has a turtleback hump in the middle. Before a subway station was plonked down on the southern end of the street several years ago, it measured 786 m long. It remains only 8 m wide, a fact that Beijing drivers blithely overlook, along with the fact it is supposed to be a one-way street with limited traffic – though increasingly dense crowds deter all but the most intrepid drivers.

The neighbourhood, in the shadow of the Drum Tower and close to both Shichahai and the Forbidden City, has long been prize real estate, with some of the finest *siheyuan* courtyard homes in the city. In Qing times, as the domain of the Bordered Yellow Banner, it was, in the words of John Minford, co-translator of *The Story of the Stone* (better known as *Dream of the Red Chamber*), 'a sort of Manchu Kensington'.

During Qianlong's reign, the prosaic hump of 'Luoguo' gave way to the more dignified, martial 'Luogu'. The many carved stone drums standing in pairs at the entryways to *siheyuan* around the neighbourhood attest to its historic population of military officials; it had previously been popular with Ming dynasty generals. Civil officials' homes featured a different style of *mendun* ('door stone') – a pair of rectangular blocks with a lion on top like an official seal, or 'chop'. Liu Yong and his fellow authors of the Chinese-language *Fifteen Lectures in Beijing History and Culture* trace the history of *mendun* back to the earliest courtyard houses of the Han dynasty; they comment that a tall red door without *mendun* is as 'tasteless' a sight as a man dressed up in a suit without shoes. While Beijing's largest extant *mendun*, 90 cm tall, can be found just inside Xizhimen, the smallest is on Ju'er Hutong itself, a tiny 15 cm in height.

The *wangfu* (princely mansion) of Prince Seng (Senggelinqin in Manchu), who led the Qing forces against the British and French in the Second Opium War, once occupied nearly the entire length of Chaodou (Fried Beans) Hutong, which branches off to the west of Nanluoguxiang. Ronglu, the powerful commander of the Imperial Guard who was rumoured to have been Cixi's childhood sweetheart and was a member of the Plain White Banner, lived in a grand residence off Ju'er itself, with a multi-courtyard mansion and extensive garden. Corresponding to today's 3, 5 and 7 Ju'er Hutong, the estate extended back to tiny Shoubi Hutong when it was still called Choupi, or 'Stinking Skin' Hutong. The 'empress' of the de-throned last emperor of China, Puyi, grew up in a residence spanning numbers 35 and 37 of nearby Mao'er Hutong.

During the Republican years, both warlords and Nationalist officials lived in the neighbourhood. The roll call of famous residents also includes the novelist Mao Dun, China's Minister for Culture from 1949–65. Mao Dun's old home on Houyuanensi (Back Garden Benevolence Temple) Hutong, one south of Ju'er, is today a museum. Though few are open to the public, dozens of the mansions around here are heritage-listed. Some have been converted to hotels or hostels.

Many more have become tenement-like *dazayuan*. The unpleasant truth of *hutong* living in the twenty-first century is the same dearth of plumbing and heating that have always been an issue with Beijing's courtyard homes, and the fact that so many of the buildings are in need of expensive renovation.

Developers hover, eager to replace ramshackle horizontals with neat verticals. Yet as Shu Yi, the son of the novelist Lao She and a preservation activist, warns: 'History is being wiped out before our eyes. Soon there will be nothing left.' He has called the *hutong* Beijing's 'second city wall'.

In 1990 Nanluoguxiang and its *hutong* were officially recognized as one of the city's top 25 historical districts. Ju'er became the site of a prize-winning architectural experiment that attempted to take the *siheyuan* and *hutong* living into a new age. But Nanluoguxiang remained a quiet neighbourhood, its ancient buildings slowly crumbling along the narrow main street with its broken cobbles.

In 2002 a photographer and pioneer of China's domestic backpacking scene fixed up one of Nanluoguxiang's semi-derelict old buildings to open the Pass-By Bar. Its casual, funky

Dazayuan courtyard in Dashila'r transformed into a pop-up shop for Beijing Design Week.

decor, featuring the owner's photographs from his travels in Tibet, unvarnished courtyard aesthetic and relatively inexpensive Western food gave it an off-the-beaten-track cachet that attracted young Beijing artists, writers and others. In the years following the establishment of the Pass-By – still a Nanluoguoxiang institution – the street morphed into a domestic and international tourist destination, where on weekends and holidays the crowds reach human-wave proportions.

Even Ju'er has sprouted shops, restaurants, backpacker hostels, a mah jong parlour and café-bars, including one run for a time by a direct descendant of the Chinese sage Mencius (372–289 BCE). Once, I stumbled upon an ad hoc school – several rooms within a *dazayuan* – where volunteers, including foreigners, taught English and maths to migrant workers.

In the years I've been around Nanluoguxiang, I've seen come and go a Tibet Café run by members of the Tibetan Khampa ethnic minority, a therapeutic massage centre staffed by former peasants from a Shaanxi province village, a nail parlour run by people from a village in Shanxi province, a Hunan restaurant run by a group of young Hunanese (who briefly changed over to Yunnan food when that was more trendy) and even a hole-in-the-wall pub run by Australians.

During the run-up to the Olympics, Nanluoguxiang was again declared a heritage site to be protected. Yet pell-mell development and apparent unconcern on the part of authorities have degraded its historic legacy. Fly-by-night businesses rip down historical facades and replace them with garishly lit storefronts constructed from plastic and plywood. Months later, the businesses are gone, but the damage remains. Opportunistic rents have forced out many of the original community businesses, such as a shop where locals queued three times a day to buy the stuffed buns, steamed breads and pan-fried flatbreads called *laobing* that are a staple on Beijing tables.

Not long after the Olympics ended, entire blocks of heritage housing on either side of the south end of the street were demolished to make way for a subway station servicing lines

6 and 8. Along with a largely silent crowd of onlookers, including many I recognized as long-time residents, I watched as workers sledgehammered the old grey wall of what days before had been a restaurant-café. Even as they smashed the plate-glass window at the front, the owner sat on a sofa inside, facing out on to the street in a stoic protest.

In *The Last Days of Old Beijing*, Michael Meyer quotes a story by Pearl Buck written in 1929. In it, an old man in the southern city of Nanjing similarly sits through the demolition of his shop:

> they took the tiles from the roof and the light began to seep down between the rafters. At last they took the rafters, and he sat there within four walls with the noonday sunshine beating on him . . . people stared at him curiously but said nothing, and he sat on.

The shopkeeper's son in the story had no time for nostalgia: 'Why, these streets were made a thousand years ago. Are we never to have new ones?'

Beijing today has no lack of new streets.

The Bell Tower today.

The Dragon's Vein

The Ming capital's north–south axis began at Qianmen, the Front Gate in the centre of the south end of Tiananmen Square. Qianmen, the city's formal entrance, was – and is – also the point from which the formal measure of distance from Beijing to anywhere else in China is calibrated. An ornamental plaque just outside Zhengyangmen, Qianmen's principal gate tower, marks the 'zero point' for highways leading out from the capital: when a place is described as x km from Beijing, it usually means it is that far from Zhengyangmen.

In the Ming and Qing dynasties, Zhengyangmen was another kind of 'zero point' – the start of the Corridor of a Thousand Steps, or Imperial Way, leading to the gate of the Imperial Precinct, Tiananmen. Considerable power resided on either side of the corridor in the form of the imperial Six Ministries: three military ministries to the west, three civil ministries to the east. The axis then passed through Tiananmen, the defensive gate Duanmen and finally the Meridian Gate (Wumen) that gives entry to the Forbidden City itself. If it could be said that power passed along the axis like a current, it surged in its approach to the main throne hall, Taihedian.

Imperial power concentrated along this axis, which was closely associated with the emperor himself. Whether officiating over a major ceremony with his court in the Taihedian, being conveyed in his yellow palanquin to the Meridian Gate to survey prisoners of war or promulgate an edict, or borne down a gold-dusted Imperial Way in a curtained cab on the back of a Burmese elephant to conduct rites at the Temple of Heaven, the emperor commanded the axial paths and the central archways of the gates. On occasion he shared the central archway of the Meridian Gate with, for example, the top graduates of the imperial examinations or honoured emissaries from foreign lands. But even the structure of the imperial palanquin, carried on the shoulders of bearers who ran on either side – never in front or behind – ensured that the emperor owned the centre.

Moving north from Taihedian, the axis progresses through another two ceremonial halls before passing through the Gate of Heavenly Purity that opens on to the residential quarters of the Forbidden City: the emperor's Palace of Heavenly Purity, the empress's Palace of Earthly Tranquillity and the Hall of Union lying between them on the axis.

Beyond the Forbidden City's Gate of Divine Prowess, it traverses the five peaks of the former imperial preserve now called Jingshan Park to reach Tiananmen's 'mirror' of Di'anmen,

Arrow Tower, Zhengyangmen, Mao Zedong Memorial Hall, Tiananmen and (just visible in the distance) Jingshan on a clear October afternoon.

the no longer extant Gate of Earthly Peace, in the north of the Imperial Precinct. Its traditional terminus is at the axially aligned Drum and Bell Towers.

When the Ming Jiajing emperor walled in the southern suburbs in the sixteenth century to protect them from Mongol raids, he extended the axis southward to the new Outer City's south gate of Yongdingmen. Before the construction of the Olympic Green for the 2008 Olympics, which extended it further northward, it measured 7.8 km from top to toe.

The prescription for the axis comes from the ancient *Canon of the Jade Ruler*, the monk Zicong's guide and inspiration for the design of the Yuan capital of Khanbalik. It aligns the capital and court with a celestial geometry that places the emperor in the position of the Pole Star. The Ming, which overthrew the Yuan, followed similar principles but, as discussed earlier, shifted their own axis to the east of that of the Yuan so that, being closer to the sun, it would ensure that the Ming's qi would suppress that of the Yuan.

It's said that a 'dragon's vein', a feng shui phenomenon associated with good fortune, runs along Beijing's axis. When Line 8 of the Beijing metro is complete, it will shoot up this vein from south of Yongdingmen to north of the Olympic Green, making only a slight eastern detour around Tiananmen Square and the Palace, a route extending 17 km in all.

Dragons also symbolize imperial power. Bas-relief dragons wend their way up the central marble 'cinnabar stone' over which the emperor, in robes embroidered with dragon motifs, was carried to his 'dragon throne' in Taihedian, the roof of which features 'dragon kisses', dragon heads that face off across the ridge of its roof. The sinuous River of Golden Waters flows in a curved path along the forecourt of Taihedian in such a way, as Hok-Lam Chan writes in *Legends of the Building of Old Beijing*, as 'to bolster the circulation of the dragon's ether'. Geomancers called Jingshan (or Longevity Hill, as it was known in the Ming) 'the back of the dragon's cave' so that, as Chan explains, it would 'conserve the auspicious ether' generated by the flow of waters and the interaction of *yin* and *yang* generated by the Son of Heaven's copulations with his palace women.

View from Drum Tower looking to the south, on a smoggy October afternoon.

The Chinese dragon, a fanciful composite of camel, cow, snake, deer and carp, may be a symbol of imperial power, but it is also a folkloric creature associated with the sometimes malevolent control of water and rain. Beijing's patron deity, Nezha, is renowned as a wrangler and conqueror of local water-controlling dragons. A Tantric boy deity with a red stomach-protector, breath of blue mist, multiple arms, a fire-tipped spear and wind-fire wheels on which he flies (making him, incidentally, the god of bus and taxi drivers) tussled with dragons that ruled the Bitter Waste Sea (the North China Plains) and visited havoc on the city's water supply. In one version of the legend, he fought a dragon who denied the city rain unless given human children to eat. Nezha stories were so popular in Yuan times the city was nicknamed Nezha Town. But during the Ming and Qing dynasties, Nezha faded into the background, no longer the staple of storytellers and plays he had been in Khanbalik.

The Nezha myth became entwined with early Ming history only in the early Republican period, when what David Der-wei Wang has characterized as 'the ghostly veil of nostalgia' shrouded the crumbling city. It is in stories published at that time, both in Chinese and by English writers including E.T.C. Werner (whose daughter's murder in 1937 is the subject of Paul French's *Midnight in Peking*), that Nezha made his comeback. The twentieth-century accounts had Nezha guiding Yongle's advisers on the layout of the Ming capital and palace. In these accounts, his head is associated with Qianmen and his shoulders, hands, outward-bent knees and feet with the other eight gates of the city. The red of the palace and Imperial Precinct walls is that of his apron. His spine is the city's axis, the *hutong* his ribs. Shichahai is his bladder, another thing to consider before swimming there (see p. 203).

Given the association of the axis with power, mythic and otherwise, it's no coincidence that Mao's portrait hangs where it does, over the central arch of Tiananmen, or that his body lies in his mausoleum astride the axis, as does the 38-m-tall obelisk Monument to the People's Heroes designed by Liang Sicheng with his wife Lin Huiyin. Among the historical incidents commemorated in the bas-reliefs on the base of the monument is the May Fourth Movement, just one of many political protests and spectacles that have taken place on, gravitated towards or strived to occupy Beijing's symbolical centre.

It was from the rostrum of Tiananmen that Mao proclaimed the establishment of the People's Republic of China in 1949, and it was from there he addressed the millions of Red Guards who attended the Cultural Revolution rallies in 1966. It was in the square and around the Monument to the People's Heroes that protestors flocked in the Tiananmen Incident of 1976, and again in 1989, when pro-democracy protesters occupied the square. National Day celebrations and military parades from 1949 to the present crescendo as they reach the axis.

Mao had hoped to reorientate the city along an alternative east–west axis, continuing the work begun by Yuan Shikai to lengthen Chang'an Avenue in both directions. In the twenty-first century, Beijing's governors added a second axis to the west, which runs through both the Millennial Monument and Beijing West Station. These axes have their functions, but lack magic.

Most days, out-of-towners gather to watch the ceremonial raising and lowering of the flag at dawn and dusk in the square, and tourists meander about taking photos. But few locals who live under the Communist Party's authoritarian regime would be unaware of the prowling masses of plain-clothes police who complement the presence of uniformed security personnel and soldiers on the square. When, from time to time, protesters manage to unfurl a banner, the time between action and reaction can be measured in seconds. Yet in October 2013 an SUV, allegedly driven by Uighur anti-government protesters, crashed through the square's security barriers and ploughed through a crowd of people, injuring dozens before exploding; five people – three in the car and two tourists – died. It would be marginally easier to protest elsewhere – but everyone knows that the further you go from that dragon's vein, that spine, that axis, the less it matters.

'Chinese Town'

When the Qing kicked the non-Bannermen Chinese residents and their businesses out of the Inner City in the seventeenth century, most moved to the walled Outer City south of Qianmen. The Outer City became the 'Chinese City', at its heart the thoroughfare of Qianmen Street, leading from the city gate down towards the Temple of Heaven in the Chinese City's southwest. By the early twentieth century Qianmen Street and its surrounding *hutong* were renowned for food, entertainment and shopping. On the one hand were countless food stalls and pedlars offering everything from *jianbing* (savoury crêpes) to ox-marrow tea with candied fruits. On the other, there were great restaurants like Quanjude, which served up its famous Peking duck roasted over the wood from fruit trees.

China's first screenings of moving pictures, or 'electric shadows' as they are still known, took place in the Outer City. China's own first film was a silent movie of a Peking Opera. The theatres offered opera, the tea houses storytelling and music, and the *hutong* a moveable feast of shadow puppetry, street acrobatics, wrestling, magic and comic dialogues. In the twisting, teeming lanes of Tianqiao, you might encounter legendary street performers such as 'Pockmark' Cao, a storyteller with a belled plait that rose from his head like an exclamation mark. You could easily lose yourself (and your money) in the district's brothels, opium dens and gambling parlours, and then pray for salvation or just better luck in its many temples. There was something for everyone, especially the inevitable standover men and gangs of pickpockets.

For a safer, more anodyne experience of Tianqiao's pleasures, a mere 20 Chinese cents bought entry to South City Amusement

The entrance to the Outer City: north end of Qianmen Street, 1900.

Park on its northwest corner. South City offered billiards and bowling, magic shows, food stalls, 'popgun' games, films, acrobats and Peking Opera – even if you'd be unlikely to catch the likes of Mei Lanfang on its carnivalesque stages.

The bookstores and curio shops, stationery shops and printing presses of Liulichang, the old glazed tile factory west of Tianqiao, meanwhile, were a magnet for the city's literati. According to the writer Wang Jie, the great early twentieth-century author Lu Xun visited Liulichang no less than 480 times, acquiring some 4,000 old books, scrolls and manuscripts.

The Japanese occupation and civil war in the 1930s and '40s brought bankruptcy and ruin to many of the area's businesses. Then, the decades of puritanism, political movements and poverty that followed the Communist victory in 1949 saw the colourful districts south of Qianmen fade to grey.

In 1980, not long after Deng Xiaoping launched the policies of economic reform and opening up, the city tore down the Ming and Qing dynasty shops of Liulichang and rebuilt them in faux-antique style. Tourists might prefer authenticity, however shabby, but tourism in post-1949 China has never really been about *them*. In Mao's day, tourism's agenda was diplomacy and propaganda. Now, the red of its agenda is that of the redback, the 100-yuan note that is China's largest banknote: unfortunately, that often translates to replacing antique structures and icons rather than conserving them: authenticity can be less important than turning a quick and easy profit.

Liulichang is still a mecca for calligraphy materials, seals, fans, picture books and the odd brass doorknocker in the shape of a lion's mouth, as busloads of tourists can attest. But you're unlikely to run into any of the city's literati there – your chances are probably better at the Apple Store at The Village shopping plaza in Sanlitun.

As part of the city's Olympics refresh, the entire down-at-heel commercial district running south from Qianmen was slated for demolition and reconstruction. The project was a management fiasco and eventually fell into the lap of the property developers of SOHO. The company, led by a husband and wife team, has been behind some of the capital's most architecturally entertaining residential and office developments. But SOHO was not experienced in conservation or traditional design. It reproduced Qianmen Street as a cut-rate 'tidy town' version of old Beijing; China's own Chinatown, lacking even the veracity featured in the Beijing Film Studio's old Beijing film set. A trolley glides down a pedestrian street lined with two- and three-storey buildings with ye olde Republican era facades and neat plantings of crab apple trees. Photogenic at a distance, disappointing in detail, Qianmen Shopping Street is a kind of upmarket, updated, open-air South City Amusement Park – a sanitized version of a lost world.

Diplomacy and propaganda still play a role in contemporary tourism: one reconstructed laneway off Qianmen Street leads to 'Alishan Square', named for a famous mountain in Taiwan. The

Qianmen Shopping Street today: a sanitized version of a lost world.

mountain is home to some of the island's aboriginal people, whose life was romanticized in the faux-folk song 'Alishande guniang' ('Girl from Alishan'). The song blasts from the speakers in Alishan Square. Given that the song was written in 1947 by a Shanghai film director in need of a quick theme song and a Sichuan composer who'd never been to Alishan, it seems an appropriate soundtrack for the incongruous little plaza, with its decorative map of Taiwan and coral and globe shops.

North end of Qianmen Shopping Street.

Hordes of provincial tourists in matching baseball caps bounce like pinballs between *lao zihao* (famous old brands) such as the Quanjude Peking duck restaurant and the *xin zihao* (famous new brands) of Starbucks, Zara and Häagen-Dazs. Occasionally they pause to take photos with the ghosts of Beijing past who are frozen in cast-bronze poses under the birdcage-shaped streetlamps. The traditional residents of the area, memorialized in slickly produced souvenir books and photographs as well as statuary, are meanwhile being pushed in ever greater numbers out into faceless high-rise, high-density piles beyond the fifth and sixth ring roads.

No Beijing residents I know ever go near the new Qianmen Street – it's not for them anyway. Some of my better-off friends do make an exception for the stylish Australian-run restaurant Capital M, on the third floor of a new-for-old building at Qianmen Street's northeastern corner. The view from Capital M's balcony takes in the top of Qianmen Street as well as Zhengyangmen with its Arrow Tower, a corner of the Mao Mausoleum, a snippet of Tiananmen and, on the clearest days, the roof of the pavilion atop Jingshan as well. To the east stands the old Qianmen railway station with its turn-of-the-century clock tower and arched entrance, now a railway museum.

Yet what are we really looking at? Both the Arrow Tower and Zhengyangmen were reconstructed after being badly damaged during the Boxer Rebellion. The German architect who supervised the rebuilding of the Arrow Tower capped the embrasures with architecturally incongruous white marble eyebrows and added European-style balustrades. The mausoleum's golden roof tiles do not make it a palace; the decorative overhangs of this interloper appear dour and stingy in comparison with the grandeur of the flying eaves of the gates afore and behind. As for the gate at Tiananmen, what we see is what China got in the discreet reconstruction of 1969. I have read that even the old railway station was moved from its original spot west of where it now stands.

In Europe, ruins such as those that exist in Rome and Greece are revered reminders of past greatness and loss. It is and always has been different in China. Even palace buildings in China tend to be made of wood, and wood burns. As Pierre Ryckmans (Simon Leys) has observed in 'The Chinese Attitude towards the Past', the permanence of Chinese culture 'is first and foremost a Permanence of Names'.

The Temple of Heaven's emblematic Ming dynasty circular hall was rebuilt after it burned down in 1889, buildings in the Forbidden City have burned down and been rebuilt and, although temples may date their origins to the Tang, few of their existing structures would be more than several centuries old and a number of them only decades. Even their statuary may be new or, as discussed in chapter Seven, originally from elsewhere.

In the Ming dynasty, a beautifully proportioned, arched, marble bridge spanned the narrow channel between the front and back lakes of Shichahai. It was called the Yinding (Silver Tael) Bridge for its resemblance to the 38-g (1.3-oz) pieces of silver that once served as monetary units. One of Beijing's most famous views in classical times was that from the high point of the bridge, of the shimmering reflection in Shichahai of the Western Hills. One fine autumn day in 2010, I strolled to Shichahai only to discover workers hammering the bridge to rubble. They were replacing it with a somewhat flatter bridge 'in Ming style' that would be wide enough for the SUVs of the Beijing plutocracy occupying some of the prime real estate around the lake. I am embarrassed to say I burst into tears – embarrassed because I failed to realize that I was weeping over a replica built in 1984 of a 1950s renovation of a Qing reconstruction of the Ming original.

Line 2, morning rush hour.

The Circle Line

It's 8:30 a.m. and the commuters on Beijing subway's Line 2 do what people do on rush-hour trains anywhere: text, read, doze or direct their morning stare at advertisements. On a screen by the door, a McCafé hot dog nestles into vivid green lettuce in a sesame bun: 'I'm lovin' it!', chirps the voiceover in English. Real estate flyers litter the seats, which, prime real estate themselves, only ever remain unoccupied for a matter of seconds. On one side of me, a suited man reads the *China Defence News*, on the other a young man in a tracksuit devours a paperback, the title of which translates as *Murder on the Mekong*; a student hangs from a strap and texts. Outside the window a zoetropic display of the delights awaiting the tourist to Japan flash past. The polite recorded voice announces the name of the coming station: the Yonghegong, Lama Temple, the former princely mansion where the Yongzheng emperor spent his youth.

Line 2 runs under the Second Ring Road, the path of the old city wall. Its stations are a mnemonic of Beijing's imperial past. Heading due West and counterclockwise, the next station is Andingmen (Peace Stabilized Gate). In Ming and Qing times troops re-entered the city through this gate when they returned from battle. (They departed via the nearby Deshengmen, Gate of Virtuous Victory.) The stop after that is Gulou, the Drum Tower and northernmost point of the Ming city's central north–south axis. Then it's forward to Jishuitan, named for the Yuan dynasty's Water Collecting Pool, terminus of the Grand Canal and today's Shichahai.

The train then zooms southward to Xizhimen, originally the second largest of all the city gates after Qianmen. It was

Xizhimen's Yuan antecedents whose discovery, recording and destruction were witnessed by both Liang Sicheng and Pierre Ryckmans when the gate itself was demolished during the Cultural Revolution. Xizhimen was nicknamed the Water Gate because it was through this gate that water was conveyed from the Jade Spring to the Forbidden City. It's now a mega-station in the midst of a confusing set of flyovers; I can't entirely blame the rocket-fuel liquor *ergoutou* I'd been drinking for the 45 minutes it took me one night, in −12°C weather no less, to get there from a Mongolian hotpot restaurant only several blocks away where I'd been dining with friends.

After Xizhimen comes Chegongzhuang, a former village just outside the wall (*zhuang* in a place name indicates village, just as *men* means gate). Chegongzhuang's feng shui made it a good site for burial. The Catholic Church might consider that the soul of the Jesuit Matteo Ricci went to Heaven, but his body went to Chegongzhuang; his restored tomb can be found on the nearby campus of the Beijing Administrative Institute (formerly the Beijing Party School). Chegongzhuang is also the stop for Beijing's top theatre dedicated to Peking Opera: the appropriately named Mei Lanfang Grand Theatre.

If Xizhimen was the Water Gate, Fuchengmen was the Coal Gate to which trudged the camel trains bringing deliveries from the mines at Mentougou. After Fuchengmen comes Fuxingmen (Revival of Prosperity Gate). Fuxingmen was not one of the nine original gates in the Ming and Qing city walls. Like its equivalent in the East City, Jianguomen (Build the Nation Gate), Fuxingmen was carved out of the wall during the Republican period to aid traffic flow along Chang'an Avenue; both got their current names following the Japanese surrender.

The station at the southwestern corner of the line is called Changchunjie (Cedar Street), named for a Ming dynasty temple. The train then heads east to Xuanwumen, site of the Ming and Qing elephant stables, but also nicknamed 'Death Gate' because it was through this gate that condemned criminals (including the scholars behind the Hundred Days' Reform of 1898) were taken to the execution grounds at Caishikou

(Vegetable Markets). Carved into the gate were the words 'too late for regrets'. It was at Xuanwumen that Johann Adam Schall von Bell built Beijing's first Catholic church, on the site of Ricci's old home.

Next up is Hepingmen (Peace Gate). This gate dates back only to 1926; it had no great watchtowers and, like Fuxingmen and Jianguomen, was created simply to help traffic flow between the Inner and Outer Cities. Following Hepingmen is the all-important Qianmen, the 'Front Gate', the only station where the gate is more than just a historical memory.

Then comes Chongwenmen, named for a classical expression meaning 'respect for civil rule'. It's also known as Hadamen after a Yuan dynasty Mongol prince, Hada, who lived nearby. Just south of the Qing's Legation Quarter, Chongwenmen was once the busiest gate in the whole city, charged with collecting the entry and exit taxes that paid for everything from Empress Dowager Cixi's cosmetics in the Qing to Yuan Shikai's salary during the Republic. Unlike at the other eight gates, at Chongwenmen closing time was announced with bells instead of gongs, and may well be why, in Beijing dialect, the term *zhongdian*, 'bell point', is used to indicate the hour. It forms a pair with Xuanwumen, a phrase signifying military glory; just as the military (*wu*) and civil (*wen*) offices were positioned on the west and east respectively, both inside and outside the palace in the Ming and Qing dynasties, so Xuan*wu*men is to Qianmen's west and Chong*wen*men to the east. Both were pulled down in 1965.

Following Chongwenmen comes the bustling Beijing Railway Station, soon after which the train heads north, pivoting at Jianguomen. Jianguomen station isn't too far from the International Post Office, itself close to the site where the Qing postal bureau was set up in 1907. The train sweeps up to Chaoyangmen, the old entry point for the city's grain shipments, and then Dongsi Shitiao, where granaries have stood since the time of the Yuan dynasty. Finally, the train pulls into Dongzhimen (East Direct Gate). Like its symmetrical partner in the west, Xizhimen, Dongzhimen has its antecedents in the Yuan. In the Ming, it was the gate through which building

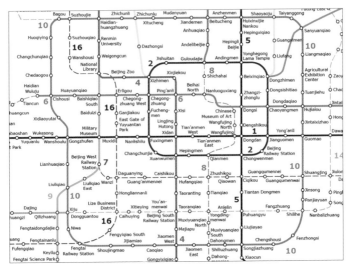

Subway map, 2014.

materials like lumber and gravel were transported. It became a well-to-do neighbourhood with some elegant princely mansions and fine courtyard houses, and is today the centre of the embassy quarter. After Dongzhimen, the train completes its circle at the Lama Temple.

Unlike the brightly coloured stations and sleek trains of Beijing's more recent subway lines, Line 2 itself, with its dim, cavernous platforms, remains a palpable link to Beijing's more distant, pre-prosperity past as well. After visiting the Soviet Union in 1949, where he was impressed by Moscow's subway, Mao decided Beijing should have one too. It was 1958 before the project got under way, codenamed Project 401. Line 1, also part of the project, was to run under the new east–west axis of the extended Chang'an Avenue. Project 401 was temporarily derailed by the economic dysfunction of the Great Leap Forward and subsequent famine. As tensions with the Soviet Union rose in the 1960s, it gained new urgency as part of a secure getaway plan for the leadership in case of nuclear attack.

Just to be sure, engineers dug a scale model of the tunnel in the desert at Lop Nor in northwestern Xinjiang, set a subway car inside, and the army dropped a 780-kg A-bomb on top. After two further years of trials that included several catastrophic fires, three fatalities and more than 100 injuries, China's first subway line, linking Beijing Train Station with Gongzhufen (Princess Tomb), 10.7 km due west, opened for organized visits in January 1971. Nixon rode it on his visit in 1972. It was formally launched in 1981; three years later, Line 2 began operation.

Riding it back then, when these were the only two lines, Beijing's subway struck me as one of the oddest and least practical of public transport systems. You could circle the inner city on the train, but never enter it. It brought to mind the fact that there was once a wall, that Beijing has always been a city of walls, of careful demarcations between *nei* (inner) and *wai* (outer). Lying just south of the ultimate demarcation, the Great Walls, Beijing's own battlements enclosed, in turn, the dusty rose-coloured walls of the Imperial Precinct. A few metres of the Imperial Precinct walls have been reconstructed as part of Dong Huangchenggen Park along Beiheyan Street. These, of course, encircled those of the Forbidden City itself.

Status determined how far inside these walls you might go. With the exception of eunuchs, no man but the emperor could penetrate the part of the Forbidden City known as *Danei*, the Great Within. Walls kept some out and confined others: women, for example, were expected to remain within the innermost quarters of palace or household. Beijing has long fostered a culture of walls that insulated and isolated as effectively as they guarded; a number of Chinese thinkers have noted their subtle influence on Chinese political thought.

The Circle Line is today but one link in a sophisticated transport network that conveys people as easily to Wangfu-jing and the old Lantern Market (Dengshikou) in the old city centre as to the Yuanmingyuan in the northwest and Marco Polo Bridge in the southwest, to the Yuan Dynasty Relics Park, the airport's new Terminal Three or the Olympic Green's Birds Nest. It has opened the closed city, and in many ways Line 2 – circular and chained by every station name to a thickly inscribed past, but now boasting so many transit points outward – seems a perfect metaphor for Beijing's own transformation.

The Thirsty City

It's China's National Day holiday, 1 October. The brimming waters of Shichahai (Ten Temple Lake), three linked lakes north of the former Imperial Precinct, sparkle under a retro-blue morning sky. Workers on low motorized skiffs are skimming leaves, plastic bags and other flotsam from the surface with long-handled nets. The area around the lakes has had a large Muslim population and a mosque since 1644; outside a lakeside halal restaurant, men in white caps serve up steamed and grilled breads with sweet or savoury fillings to queuing locals. The trishaws – bicycle rickshaws – are already milling at Yinding (Silver Tael) Bridge. A louche young driver rises on his pedals and calls out to me in English: 'Lady! *Hutong* tour!' I shoot back a smartarse answer in Chinese. In Beijing, verbal banter is a folk art. He laughs and gives me the thumbs up.

In a few hours Shichahai will be swarming with Chinese and foreign tourists. They'll wander along its willow-fringed paths, paddle boats on the lakes, troop through Prince Gong's Mansion (see pp. 231–7) and throng the restaurants and souvenir shops. When a few short months later the lakes freeze over and temperatures swoop below zero, the young and hardy will return to sled and skate. But for now, everyone's busy soaking up the last burst of summery warmth before autumn sets in. When darkness falls, it'll still be balmy, and the open-fronted bars standing doorjamb-to-doorjamb on the lakeshore will crank up their warring sound systems, the touts launching a barrage of temptations on passersby – Beer! Rock 'n' roll! Girls!

In 2003 the SARS epidemic scared the city's clubbers away from the packed venues around the Workers Stadium and

Morning at Shichahai.

nearby Sanlitun (Three Mile Village). Bars closed (temporarily) in the city only to regroup at Shichahai, previously one of the most peaceful places in Beijing. Early in the morning, when it remains the domain of the locals, it still is.

At a pocket park, middle-aged people perform calisthenics to pop music burbling from a tinny radio and a young man swings purposefully along the monkey bars, his bare arms sinuous. Further west and across the narrow lakeside street, stands a grand residence adjacent to the mansion of Prince Chun (father of Puyi, the last Qing emperor) that was once part of its garden. The widow of the republican revolutionary Sun Yat-sen and a former president of the People's Republic of China, Song Qingling, lived there from 1963 until her death in 1981; it's now a museum to her memory. Shichahai has long been one of Beijing's best addresses.

Following the curvature of the lake, in another tiny park, I come upon a pack of dog fanciers discussing the apnoea afflicting their Pekinese, the 2,000-year-old breed of 'sleeve dogs' (pets small enough to be carried in one's sleeve) once favoured by the imperial court. Further along, an old man carefully hooks his bird cage on to a tree branch as his neighbour confides that though her marriage was passionless, at least her husband never hit her – and he always handed over his pay packet. (Like most novelists, I'm an incorrigible eavesdropper.)

Some of Beijing's greatest delights are its constructed lakes and waterways. These include extant segments of the old Grand Canal, Kunming Lake at the Summer Palace and Fuhai at Yuanmingyuan, as well as Beihai (North Lake), to which the lakes of Shichahai are linked. Even the Yuan Dynasty Relics Park, tracing the remains of the northern section of Khanbalik's city wall, runs alongside a renovated section of the Yuan dynasty city moat which leads in the east to Beijing's largest surviving marsh, bursting with water lilies and bulrushes.

In historical times, Beijing was famous for the abundant sweetness of its well water. A thousand years ago there was enough well water for residents to tend their orchards of fruit, date and chestnut trees – the produce from which ranked highly in the Tang court. Nezha had done well in his battle with the Dragon King for supremacy over the area's water supply; the Dragon King was confined to Zhongnanhai and Beihai (Nezha's stomach), obediently 'lifting his head' a few times a year to bring spring and summer rains. As late as the Qing dynasty, the Jade Spring in the Western Hills provided much of Beijing's water via the reservoir of Kunming Lake. The writer Lin Yutang described Shichahai in the Republican period as 'half rice fields and half lotus ponds'. Though drier than it had been, say, in the Tang, the city the Communists took over in 1949 was blessed with abundant marshlands, ponds and streams.

A small part of Shichahai, severed by the Ming city walls, existed as a small reed pool until 1958, when the city government dredged it and gave it the name Taipinghu (Peace Lake).

Covered in lotus blossoms and humming with frogs, it was one of author Lao She's favourite retreats – and the scene of his still mysterious death. Today Taipinghu is a marketplace and train depot. The Jade Spring has run dry. So have the wells, though they'd already lost their famous sweetness by 1885.

The elderly physicist Wang Zhidong remembered visiting his grandfather's home near the Goldfish Ponds, a naturally replenishing pool south of Qianmen where ornamental fish were bred for sale. Wang told an interviewer for the Canadian environmental foundation Probe International that when he was a university student, the

> whole western area of Beijing was water . . . there were reed beds everywhere. If you walked in from Haidian South Road it was all just a crescent-shaped reed pond, with the reeds growing as tall as a man.

When Wang began teaching at the Beijing Institute of Industry in 1951, the Gaoliang River that once carried Cixi's imperial barge to the Summer Palace flowed past the institute. That river has become a trickle; the Goldfish Ponds are gone. Of Beijing's 200-odd rivers and streams, most have dried up. Professor Wang said he could never have imagined that water supply would become such a major problem for Beijing, professing himself 'really worried for the next generation'.

Seeing people fishing and swimming at Shichahai, I worry for this one. The surface beauty of the lake is deceptive: on holidays, its waters are replenished from the Guanting reservoir – a water source so polluted that it hasn't been used as a source of drinking water since 1997. Guanting is one of two reservoirs out of dozens built in the 1950s that are still in use. The other one, Miyun, was operating at one-tenth its capacity in 2012, and is also contaminated, but not as badly. The city has no natural source of clean drinking water left. It siphons up so much water from its underground karst aquifers (3 billion cubic metres of groundwater a year), that its water table is dropping fast and the land subsiding. Much of the water it uses is piped in from what the historian and environmental activist Dai

Qing, writing in the *New York Review of Books* in 2007, called 'increasingly resentful' neighbouring provinces. She recalled her father-in-law Wang Sen, the hydrologist charged with constructing the Guanting reservoir in 1953, saying: 'Build a dam, bleed a river dry.'

The demands of industry and a growing population are part of the story. In a 76-page report, Probe International also cites a string of 'short-sighted policies' as culprits. These include draining wetlands, deforestation and over-reliance on dams (especially environmentally disastrous black rubber dams). What's more, as late as 2012, households were charged a mere 3 yuan – less than 50 U.S. cents – a tonne for water use, with no penalties for wasteful consumption.

In 2007, according to Probe, Beijing people had access to less than 230 cubic metres of water per person – one-thirtieth of the world average, one-eighth of the Chinese average, and less than one-quarter of what they enjoyed per capita in 1949. It is also, as Dai Qing notes, less than a quarter of the amount of water sucked up by a typical eighteen-hole golf course in one day.

That's not a frivolous comparison. Thanks to the sport's popularity among China's business and political elite since the 1990s, dozens of golf courses have sprung up around Beijing, many with multiple water features and covering more than 8,100 ha of land. According to the Beijing Water Authority, golf courses swallowed up 40 million cubic metres of water in 2012; at least six were forced to close in 2013. Dai Qing cites the vast ornamental lake surrounding the National Centre for the Performing Arts in central Beijing and the Shunyi Water Park (built on the dry bed of the Chaobai River) as among Beijing's other 'water follies'.

Since the 1970s Beijing has experienced over 25 years of drought. An average of 590 mm of rain falls on the city annually, just over half of what New York, which sits on the same latitude, can expect. Shanghai receives over twice as much. Local farmers struggle to secure enough water for their crops. Drought is not a new problem: 'I have reigned for fifty-seven years,' the Qing Kangxi emperor lamented,

'and have conducted rain-prayers for almost fifty years!'
The water shortage, however, is unprecedented.

What Beijing lacks in water, it makes up for in dust. This too is not an entirely new problem. In his 1907 *Indiscreet Letters from Peking*, Bertram Lenox Simpson wrote (under his pen name B. L. Putnam Weale) that Beijing's dust was 'distinguished among all the dusts of the earth for its blackness, its disagreeable insistence in sticking to one's clothes, one's hair, one's very eyebrows'. The worst dust storms occur in spring, when the Gobi Desert in the Mongolian lands north of the Great Walls blows tonnes of mineral-laden sand on Beijing in candy-coloured tempests that can last hours, blotting out the sun and grounding flights. As more open-cut mines are gouged into the grasslands of Inner Mongolia, the storms have become toxic. The city's air is already so polluted that it is frequently

The River of Golden Waters at the Forbidden City.

considered hazardous by international standards, and in early 2013 and 2014 was so dire that it made international headlines as well. The Beijing Municipal Health Bureau reported in late 2013 that the incidence of lung cancer in the capital increased by more than 50 per cent in ten years, though it blamed cigarette smoking as the primary cause. The municipal government announced a 'Heavy Air Pollution Contingency Plan' that would close schools and curb traffic, among other measures, following any three consecutive days of 'serious pollution'. In early 2014, scientists warned that the effect of the smog on crops was comparable to a 'nuclear winter'.

Beijing has an ambitious and successful programme of grey-water recycling, and a number of water-intensive industries have been forced out of the city. Local farmers too have been switching to less thirsty crops. There are controversial plans for further diversion of water from both the Yellow and Yangtze rivers and for energy-intensive desalination plants that won't work in winter when the sea closest to Beijing freezes over.

Meanwhile, it never rains but it pours. The capital experienced its heaviest downpour in 60 years in a single 24-hour period in July 2012. Floodwaters surged down streets and submerged highways, claiming dozens of lives, destroying over 8,000 homes, causing billions of yuan in damage and exposing a gaping lack of attention to the city's drainage infrastructure. I wrote to a friend living in a courtyard house in one of Beijing's remaining *hutong* neighbourhoods (see pp. 173–9) to ask how she'd fared. She replied that the courtyard house had stood up well to the storm; her neighbourhood had been saved, she said, by the drainage provided by its ancient moats and canals. There may be some kind of lesson there.

On the Art Trail

By the late 1990s the outmoded electronics factories of sector 798 in the old Bauhaus-style military-industrial complex at Jiuxianqiao (Drunken Fairy Bridge) were struggling to keep afloat in the increasingly competitive, market-driven economy. In 2001 they began allowing artists to rent space in 798 for studios, living spaces and galleries. The cavernous workshops, some with Cultural Revolution era slogans still visible on the walls, made ideal backdrops for exhibitions of the studiously ironic 'political pop' that was trope *du jour*.

By 2003 sector 798 boasted over 400 galleries and a listing in *Time* magazine as one of the world's top 25 art centres. But rising rents and what artist and critic Yin Ji'nan famously described in 2004 as an artistic 'petting zoo' atmosphere eventually drove most cutting-edge artists further afield. Some, including Ai Weiwei, one of the first into 798, moved to nearby Caochangdi Village. But the taming of 798 suited the municipal government. Beginning in 2008, with an eye on its tourism potential, the city government invested over 100 million yuan in infrastructure for the arts district. By 2010, 798 was drawing more than 2 million visitors, one-third of whom were foreigners. It has become as much a site to shop, eat and play as it is a place to view art.

The scene at Jiuxianqiao, Caochangdi and other 'art districts' or 'art villages' in Beijing continues to evolve. Within the same complex as 798 is 751 D•Park, a decommissioned coal gas plant. By the second decade of the new millennium 751 D•Park had become a hub for industrial, interior and fashion design, and a popular venue for fashion shows, 'Design Week' activities and international product launches alike.

798 Space gallery with Cultural Revolution slogans on the ceiling: 'Long Live Chairman Mao!'

Beijing's highly commercialized art scene is a long way from the original, amateur spirit of Chinese art. In imperial times, a mastery of calligraphy, poetry and brush painting was the mark of the gentleman-scholar. Wang Xizhe's *Preface to the Poems Composed at the Orchid Pavilion* presented an ideal vision of that world. Wang and his friends, all talented scholar-officials, had gathered in the year 353 at a pavilion by a winding stream to drink and compose poetry. They floated wine cups on the water. Whenever one bumped against the side, the nearest person composed a verse on the spot. The *Preface* is a profoundly beautiful meditation on the fleeting nature of life and joy and its calligraphy is considered among the greatest works of Chinese art ever made. A seventh-century Tang emperor buried it with him in his tomb near Xi'an, commissioning several copies first. Over the centuries, artists have created numerous tributes to the *Preface* and the occasion that inspired it.

The eighteenth-century Qianlong emperor, one of the most energetic art collectors in history, had a passion for the *Preface*. He acquired some of the earliest Tang dynasty copies as well as the most magnificent of the artworks inspired by it, including paintings, jade carvings and calligraphy, for his collection in the Forbidden City. Qianlong even constructed his own 'Flowing Cup Pavilion', complete with an artificial winding stream, within the palace itself. Despite decades of looting and destruction, Beijing's Palace Museum still boasts an extraordinary art collection. Several years back, the large gallery above the Meridian Gate put on a superb exhibition of works collected by Qianlong relating to Wang Xizhe's masterpiece. It was a glimpse of a world that celebrated art, poetry and friendship above all else.

But if today's art scene seems at times to be about money above all else, it's good to recall that its own relatively recent antecedents are more Orchid Pavilion than auction house. From 1949 the Communist Party ordered art to serve the revolution. Yet even at the height of the Cultural Revolution, a small group of Beijing artists adhered to the ideals of beauty, friendship and art for its own sake. They painted quietly around the lakes at Shichahai and elsewhere when all around was politically orchestrated murder and madness.

The No-Names, as they called themselves, could not even have imagined exhibiting their art, much less selling it. They were an inspiration to others, including a group of young artists who came together in 1978, two years after the end of the Cultural Revolution. A number of them were associated with the samizdat publication *Today*, which held gatherings at the Yuanmingyuan, then an unreconstructed and unguarded ruin where people drank, declaimed poetry and celebrated the still-dangerous notion of self-expression. The artists called themselves the Stars to assert their place in a cosmos previously dominated by one Great Red Sun, as Chairman Mao was known. Their number included Ai Weiwei and others whose names still resonate in the Chinese art world today.

The Stars applied to the official Beijing Artists Association for permission to hold an exhibition. Nearly a year passed without news. Early in the morning on 27 September 1979, they descended on a narrow park flanking the China Art Gallery (today's National Art Museum of China) with their work. In just over an hour, they'd mounted a guerrilla exhibition of 150 works on the park fence. Word of mouth attracted huge crowds – and the interest of the Public Security Bureau, which closed it down the following day. Days later, on crutches, the woodcut artist Ma Desheng, who'd been denied entry to art school on account of physical disability, led the Stars in a defiant and international headline-grabbing march down Chang'an Avenue under a banner demanding 'democracy and artistic freedom'. They were given permission to hang their work in Beihai Park in late November 1979 and in August 1980, at the China Art Gallery itself.

Jiang Feng, then the chairman of the China Artists' Association, reportedly said at the time: 'When [the Stars] realize that the mass of the people don't understand their work, they will learn and change their ways.' I was one of an estimated 200,000 visitors (the overwhelming majority of whom were Chinese) who mobbed the gallery that summer to view the audacious works on show. But Jiang Feng had got it backwards: it was the Stars who changed everything else.

The exhibition turned out to be a seminal moment in the development of China's contemporary art scene.

Back then, there were no commercial galleries. Security forces regularly shut down shows held in public spaces like schools. Yet the scene attracted the diplomats, journalists and others in Beijing's small foreign community, for it offered them a congenial, bohemian, even outlaw alternative to the official China of stilted banquets and limited social contacts. And so diplomats, journalists and others bought this 'unofficial' art, hosted exhibitions, talked up the art abroad and helped the artists to exhibit and travel overseas. Their particular excitement about art that carried social and political messages or contained recognizably 'Chinese' imagery undeniably influenced the sort of art being produced.

Li Xianting, editor of *Fine Arts in China* – the authoritative Beijing journal of record on art trends in China from 1985 to 1989 – and a renowned champion of the scene, was critical of foreigners' judgments, noting 'they tend to be attracted to anything that is "unofficial".' Whenever I visited Li in his cramped quarters in a *dazayuan* by Shichahai, this champion of 'unofficial' art was always also keen to point out the ferment and experimentation taking place in the academies during those years as well.

Though there were other, regional hubs of artistic creativity in the 1980s, the opportunities Beijing offered for mutual contact and wider recognition made the capital a magnet for artists from the provinces. Recognizing opportunity, residents of Fuyuan Village at the old western gate of the Yuanmingyuan rented rooms to those without official permission to reside in the capital; contemporary art stars Fang Lijun and Guo Jian were among those who lived for a time in what became known as the Yuanmingyuan Artists' Village.

In February 1989 Li Xianting helped curate a landmark exhibition of Chinese avant-garde art at the China Art Gallery. The exhibition, called 'No U-Turn', involved 186 artists from all over China and nearly 300 works, including Huang Yong Ping's '*The History of Chinese Painting' and 'A Concise History of Modern Art' after Two Minutes in a Washing Machine* and a giant cross

Wang Guangyi's *Our Workers are Strong*, a sculpture at 798.

made of condoms by the Gao Brothers. When the artists Tang Song and Xiao Lu opened fire with live ammunition on their installation *Dialogue*, the police closed the exhibition. It re-opened, closed again because of a bomb threat (later alleged to be another performance artwork) and reopened again.

It was not long after that the protest movement erupted and students demonstrating for democracy raised the banner of the 'No U-Turn' exhibition as a political statement. Following the violent suppression of the movement on 3–4 June, Li Xianting and teachers at the Central Academy of Art, whose students had created a giant 'Goddess of Democracy' statue for Tiananmen Square, fell under intense investigation. A number of artists had already left China in the difficult years of the early 1980s; now a second wave fled overseas. 'The modern art of the 1980s', the critic Huang Zhuan observed, 'disappeared almost overnight.'

It came back to life in the early 1990s, when Deng Xiaoping allowed market forces freer rein in the Chinese economy. The Australian Brian Wallace, who had been living in Beijing from the 1980s, had studied at the Central Academy of Art and organized temporary exhibitions of the new Chinese art in 1988 and 1989, saw his chance. In 1992, with the assistance of the Chinese Bureau for the Preservation of Cultural and Historic Relics, he opened China's first commercial gallery,

Red Gate, in the spectacular Dongbianmen watchtower of the old Outer City wall. Although Beijing today has too many commercial galleries to count, Red Gate and Wallace remain important players, even running an international programme of residencies for artists and curators. China's growth into both an economic powerhouse and global art superpower draws artists from around the world to Beijing to work, exhibit and simply experience the scene. When, in 1985, Robert Rauschenberg became the first major contemporary artist to exhibit at the China Art Gallery, it created a sensation. In 2012, when Damien Hirst showed at a gallery in 798, it was just another (highly) notable exhibition in a crowded arts calendar that includes such major show-and-sell events as the Beijing Art Fair held each spring at the Agricultural Exhibition Hall.

Many of the Beijing artists who emigrated in previous decades, meanwhile, have returned to live and work there. The artist Guan Wei, who is now an Australian citizen, is one. In 2013 he suggested why when he summed up the scene to *Artlink* magazine as 'chaotic, fast-paced, exciting, fun and risk-taking'.

Excitement aside, there are studios in the Beijing area that would be the envy of many artists around the world in terms

The artist Ah Xian's studio in Songzhuang.

Performance art at the opening of a private art museum in Tongxian county.

of rental price and size. Over the course of a decade, the village of Songzhuang alone has attracted an incredible 4,000 artists. Living among them, fondly nicknamed the 'Village Chief', is the art writer, editor and curator Li Xianting.

In 2006, at an auction in Beijing, the original, bullet-holed installation *Dialogue* from 'No U-Turn' sold for more than U.S. $200,000. That year, Sotheby's and Christie's between them passed some $22 million worth of contemporary Asian art under the hammer. The following year, contemporary artist Liu Xiaodong set a record for a sale in China when one of his works went for $8.2 million – yet still only one-tenth of the $83.2 million paid in England in 2010 for a single Qianlong era vase.

The Nest, the Cube, the Underpants and the Egg

On the day after the British owner of Segway Inc., Jimi Heselden, died riding his gyroscopically balanced 'personal transporter' off the edge of a cliff, I happened to be visiting the Beijing National Stadium, or 'Bird's Nest'. I'd seen a report on Heselden's accidental death in the news. When I discovered a handful of people executing stately slaloms around witch's hats on Segways there, I thought I'd stumbled on an eccentric tribute to the man.

It turned out that renting Segways to tourists to ride in the stadium is one of the strategies for recouping the building's cripplingly high maintenance costs, which may reach $30 million a year. Visitor numbers to the Bird's Nest have been in steady decline since the end of the 2008 Olympics and Paralympics. Although some 100 major events, including the Italian Super Cup and 2013 International Ski Federation Freestyle World Cup, have been held there between 2008 and 2013, it remains by and large an empty nest. The national football (soccer) team declined an invitation to make it their home base and other ideas, such as transforming the iconic structure into a hotel, have failed to excite much interest.

While I was there, so far as I could see, I was the only person who was not either an employee of the stadium or propelling a Segway over the same track where Usain Bolt had set his world record. It was lonely in those stands built to accommodate 91,000 (including 80,000 in fixed seating). Despite it being a beautiful, blue-sky autumnal day, ideal for sightseeing, the Olympic Plaza outside the stadium felt only slightly less desolate. The Ling Long Pagoda, the on-site broadcast centre, beamed The Beatles''Let It Be' through

The Bird's Nest (National Stadium).

loudspeakers at the tight clumps of provincial and Taiwanese tourists being herded by their guides from the Bird's Nest to the 'Water Cube' (the National Aquatics Center) and finally over to a vast food tent. I followed them there, sampling 'authentic Beijing treats' for two to four times what I would pay outside the park in authentic Beijing itself.

The Segway is at once admirable, touching and ridiculous. A similar blend of flair and folly are evoked by the charmingly tangled Bird's Nest, designed by Herzog & de Meuron with Ai Weiwei, and the effervescent Water Cube (strictly speaking a Water Cuboid), with its hi-tech transparent cladding and solar-heated pools. Along with the Ling Long tower, which looks like a Chinese pagoda as imagined by the Jetsons, these landmark buildings sit as though dropped on the colossal expanse of the immaculate Olympic Green like big, shiny children's toys on a playroom floor.

The great architectural monuments of Beijing's imperial
past such as the Forbidden City and the lost pleasance of the
Yuanmingyuan, though covering huge tracts of land, were,
along with their designed landscapes, human in scale. They
had nothing of the monumentalism of the 'hyperbuildings'
that are the signature works of Beijing's new architecture.

Many of the new landmarks, like the Bird's Nest and the
Water Cube, have attracted nicknames, not all complimentary.
The 'Big Underpants' is how Beijing people refer to the new

The Water Cube (Beijing National Aquatics Center).

headquarters of China Central Television (CCTV) on the East Third Ring Road. Rising just south of the site of King Zhao's Golden Tower and the Line 10 subway station Jintaixizhao, the Big Underpants glows resolutely silver. It was designed by Rem Koolhaas, tagged 'the Master of Bigness' by architectural critic Martin Filler, with the urban architectural partnership OMA.

OMA had never previously designed a high-rise. Yet it is one of the largest tall buildings ever built, with more than

473,000 sq. m of floor space. Its architects utilized construction processes never tried before; the Beijing authorities, who can make such decisions unencumbered by the consultation processes that might hamper such a project in democratic countries, gave it their blessings. The *Asian Wall Street Journal* has quoted OMA director Ole Scheeren as acknowledging, 'A project like this would be impossible to do anywhere else in the world.' Martin Filler describes the result as a 'vertiginously off-kilter' building and a 'tour de force of high-tech engineering' that displays 'gravity-defying bravado'. Scheeren, who has an unusual conception of *hutong*, has elsewhere characterized it as 'a huge *hutong* in the sky'.

The unique circulation system of this two-legged structure allows 2,000 visitors to tour the national television facility daily without disturbing any of the 10,000 people who work there. In *Tide Players* the Beijing writer Zha Jianying calls it 'an ultra-futuristic, transparent piece of architecture designed by Rem Koolhaas to house the ultra-conservative, opaque headquarters of Chinese state media.'

When officials tried to give the knickers-in-a-twist structure a more dignified nickname, they settled on the fatally earnest 'Zhichuang' (Window on Knowledge). It took the people of Beijing, gold-medallists in wordplay, only as long as it takes to write a *weibo* (microblog) post to switch the characters for *zhichuang* to those of a homonym meaning haemorrhoid.

OMA also designed a 234-m-tall Beijing Television Cultural Centre that would house a five-star Mandarin Hotel next door to the, er, Window on Knowledge, as part of a larger complex. During the Chinese New Year celebrations of 2009, illegal fireworks accidentally set the unfinished hotel dramatically ablaze. This was not seen as a good omen for the coming year; under high-level orders not to transmit photos of the inferno, CCTV neglected to report on the story until social media had broadcast the story, complete with images, far and wide.

Another of Beijing's great 'hyperbuildings' is the National Centre for the Performing Arts, 'The Egg', a translucent glass-and-titanium ellipsoid dome set in a reflecting pool – yolk and albumen. Speaking to Ron Gluckman of *Asiaweek* in 2001, its

The Beijing Television Cultural Centre and the Mandarin Hotel ablaze, 2009.

French architect, Paul Andreu, whose background was largely in designing airport terminals, called this commission 'the big chance of my life'.

The government invited Andreu to lay his Egg, the size of four football pitches, on a site southwest of the Forbidden City that was one of Beijing's oldest *hutong* neighbourhoods. It incited controversy from the start. At 56 m high, it violated the zoning laws for the vicinity of the Forbidden City. More than 100 Chinese architects signed a letter protesting its construction. It would not have been nearly as contentious had it been located elsewhere – even if to the Chinese eye it also looks inauspiciously like a giant tumulus, a grave mound of supra-imperial proportions.

For better or worse, the Nest, the Cube, the Underpants and the Egg are among contemporary Beijing's landmark buildings. There are other fine examples of both large- and smaller-scale new architecture in the city. The Japanese architect Kuma Kengo's Opposite House, a chic boutique hotel with international A-list clientele, is one. Another is 'Split House', designed by Yung Ho Chang, founder of the first private architecture firm in city and the son of the designer of the National Museum of Revolution and History; Split House is one of the pavilions of the architectural showcase hotel, Commune at the Great Wall. Zaha Hadid's Galaxy SOHO residential and office complex opened in late 2012 in Beijing's East Second Ring Road's new transportation and business zone, the city's fourth CBD and the first dedicated centre for foreign businesses. Anthony Tao, of the irreverent website Beijing Cream, characterizes it as a 'weird, shiny, spaceship-like gob of postmodernity'; Hadid describes Beijing as 'a very exciting territory' for architects.

For every interesting or exceptional building there are acres of humdrum piles of concrete and glass, some Morse-coded with the odd dot or dash of colour. Then there are the buildings

'The Egg' with the nesting box of the Great Hall of the People in the background.

that have slapped together so many disparate architectural styles that they look like a man in an ill-fitting suit with clown shoes and a baseball cap. These have precedent in the great architectural conservationist Liang Sicheng's one regrettable contribution to post-1949 architecture: a 'national style' created at the behest of the Party that tacks a Chinese 'hat', a roof with curved eaves and other broadly traditional features, atop an otherwise undistinguished block. Contemporary Beijing architecture, in short, is an omnishambolic mishmash that in parts, as Martin Filler writes, makes '1980s Houston seem like Haussmann's Paris'.

Not all of the blame goes to the designers. Hong Kong architect Tao Ho wanted his China Construction Bank in Beijing wrapped in translucent green glass; the developers ignored this, choosing instead what the writer Ron Gluckman in *Asiaweek* dubs 'Darth Vader-type dark glass'. Gluckman quotes the dismayed Tao Ho as saying 'the difference is night and day' and says that Chang'an Avenue itself has

Beijing skyline with the Forbidden City in mid-frame.

acquired the nickname 'Architectural Hall of Shame' for its 'row after row of kitschy flash' displaying 'little sense of subtlety or substance'.

Aesthetics aside, Jasper Becker reports in *The City of Heavenly Tranquillity* that the reflected sunlight from the new walls of glass and mirrors have heated the asphalt to record highs in summer, and the typhoon-speed winds that can gust through the valleys between buildings have blown workers off their scaffolding, resulting in injury and death. Does anyone care? Martin Filler summarizes Koolhaas's manifesto 'Bigness, or the Problem of Large' (1994) thus:

> Beyond a certain critical mass, a building becomes a Big Building. Through size alone, such buildings enter an amoral domain, beyond good or bad. Their impact is independent of their quality . . . Bigness is no longer part of any urban tissue. It exists; at most, it coexists. Its subtext is *fuck* context.

A Taste of the City

When I think of eating home cooking in Beijing, I think of simple yet mouth-watering staples such as *laobing*, a savoury flatbread; flattened fried rolls stuffed with meat known as *jianbing*; noodles; steamed dumplings dipped in black vinegar and eaten with cloves of raw garlic; simple stir-fries; and a small bowl of millet porridge to wash it all down. Traditional Beijing tastes are for wheat and millet over rice, for mutton or lamb (eschewed as too gamey by many southerners), and for pungent, garlicky flavours.

Southerners, whether Cantonese, Shanghainese or other-ese, typically complain that northern fare is rough, unrefined, over-powering, more suitable for peasant palates than city tastes. This doesn't bother anyone in Beijing, where people boast of being *kouzhong*, 'heavy in the mouth'. Millet and wheat are northern crops and the pastoral lands north of the Great Walls are good for raising sheep and cows. The Mongolians gave Beijing its favourite winter meal of *shuanyangrou*, mutton (or Mongolian) hotpot and its refreshing summer drink of cool, sweetened yoghurt. Uighurs from Xinjiang grill the spiced kebabs that are a standard late-night snack and the Manchus have contributed a variety of treats including the classic sweet *lüdagun*, 'donkey does a somersault', glutinous millet flour scrolled around a sweetened bean paste. In fact, many of Beijing's favourite foods are not Chinese at all, at least not in an ethnic sense.

Those that are belong to the regional cuisine known as *Lu*, the classical name for nearby Shandong province. *Lu* is one of four major cuisines in China, the others being *Chuan* (Sichuan), *Huaiyang* (Shanghai area) and *Yue* (Cantonese). A friend in the

Mongolian hotpot.

Peking Opera likens the four dominant Chinese cuisines to the four main role types in Peking Opera. Spicy, fierce Sichuan food equates to the *jing*, in which the face is painted into a wild mask. Shanghai-area food, nuanced, beautiful, delicate and clever, is the *dan*, the female characters. My friend doesn't care much for Cantonese food, classing it with the *chou*, roughly translated as clowns, who in the opera context represent the wit and wiles of the lower classes. As for *Lu*, it is basic, straightforward, sometimes a little rough around the edges, but reliable: your classic *sheng*, or male role.

The imperial kitchen, of course, was another story. It's said that the Empress Dowager Cixi, having heard that in hard times the peasants were reduced to eating crude buns of steamed maize, wished to sample these for herself. As concocted by her chefs as an *amuse-bouche*, the tiny, fine-grained *wowotou* were quite nice, especially when consumed as part of a meal that might also include turtle soup, roast pork, bear's paw, shark's fin, duck webs in mustard and up to 108 other delicacies from around the empire; she couldn't see what the problem was.

Curiosity worked both ways. When it became known in the Ming dynasty that the emperor enjoyed noodles as delicate

Chef at Quanjude expertly carving duck.

as the hair on a dragon's beard, fine 'dragon-beard noodles' established themselves as a popular local dish.

No Beijing dish is as famous as Peking duck, the 1864 creation of the Qianmen chef Yang Quanren, who invented the open, 'hung oven' for roasting ducks and fed the fire with the smokeless wood of date, peach and pear trees. (Legend has it the restaurant began in an old fruit shop.) His restaurant, Quanjude, has since grown into a chain with dozens of affiliates across China and Beijing selling 2 million ducks (as well as zillions of the thin pancakes, cut shallots, cucumbers and dabs of plum sauce that complete the dish) to 5 million customers a year. Speciality Peking duck restaurants like Quanjude offer 'duck banquets', which may include fried duck hearts, boiled duck livers, mustardy duck webs – pretty much everything but the feathers. In 1985, when I was living in Beijing, another Peking duck restaurant became one of the first, if not the very first, restaurants in the city to home deliver; the duck came complete with a chef who carved it into 108 auspicious pieces right in your own home.

Possibly because of their city's long, ethnically mixed and relatively cosmopolitan history, Beijing diners are particularly open to other regional cuisines. It was not long after the first privately run restaurants opened in the 1980s that eateries featuring Sichuan and Hunan food opened up and were instantly thronged. Southwestern Yunnan and Guizhou provinces, with their piquant combinations of sweet, sour and red-hot spicy tastes, have enjoyed fads in more recent years, as have Korean, Thai and Japanese food.

With an increasingly sophisticated, cashed-up and gastronomically curious population and a growing and wealthy expatriate community, it's unsurprising that Beijing today offers a wide range of good non-Asian restaurants as well: Spanish tapas bars, Argentinian grills, Italian trattoria, French bistros, Israeli delis, Persian dining rooms and all manner of fusion, not to mention a full-fat selection of American fast-food chains. As for those nighttime food markets at Wangfujing full of scorpions and starfish – strictly for tourists, foreign and domestic.

Since the eruption, from around 2008, of a series of shocking food scandals such as those involving melamine in milk, toxic additives in pork and 'gutter' (recycled) oil in the woks, Chinese friends in Beijing have become far more selective when eating out. At the very least, they're sure to check the signs that are usually displayed at the front and

A vendor of *jianbing*, a kind of savoury crêpe.

that reveal the health inspectors' most recent report card: as in school, it's best to try for all As.

Yet in *hutong* neighbourhoods you'll still find people queuing at hole-in-the-wall shops or mobile carts for *zhima shaobing*, dense, dark sesame buns, pale, steamed *mantou* wheat buns and other staples, not to mention the ultimate Beijing comfort food, *jianbing* – thin griddle cakes topped with egg, seasoned with coriander and savoury spreads and wrapped around a crispy fried pastry, eaten any time of day. And where the *hutong* have disappeared, Beijing supermarkets almost always feature a special section offering takeaway versions of all these favourite, very *Lu*-style snacks and staples such as pulled noodles, *laobing* and more. One day, I was returning to the courtyard house where I often stay, nibbling on a *laobing* from the local supermarket. One of my neighbours saw me. 'Where did you get that?', she asked. 'The supermarket', I replied. She wrinkled her face in disgust. 'You don't know what sort of ingredients they use', she said. I replied mildly

Buying sliced melon in Dashila'r.

that it tasted all right to me. 'You like *laobing*,' she said, 'I'll
make you *laobing*.' Such neighbourly generosity is part of
what defines the city's character for me.

But perhaps the ultimate Beijing speciality is *douzhi*, a
greyish, viscous mass of fermented mung bean powder, more
gloop than soup, that's stewed in a wok and has a sour flavour
enhanced by spicy or savoury condiments. *Douzhi* is reputed
to be particularly nutritious, full of vitamin C and protein. And
its pedigree is impeccable: it dates back to the tenth century,
when the Khitan Liao ruled the place. A saying has it that 'if
you don't like *douzhi*, you're not a real Beijing person.'

I was finishing this essay back in Sydney when I encountered
a woman originally from Tianjin, a city very close to Beijing.
I told her I'd just returned from Beijing. Unprompted, she asked
me if I'd ever eaten *douzhi*, and made a face. I said yes, and that
I liked it. She burst out laughing at the improbability of this:
'Only real Beijing people can stomach that stuff.'

The Prince's Garden

Down the end of a willow-fringed lane off Shichahai's Qianhai (Front Lake), at 17 Qianhai Road West, is the entrance, as the popular saying has it, to 'half the history of the Qing dynasty': Gong Wangfu, Prince Gong's Mansion. Its extensive, landscaped grounds, which cover an area of some 61,000 sq. m, are graced with elegantly proportioned buildings, covered walkways, artificial hills, lakes, a private opera theatre and follies such as one gate built to resemble a crenellated section of the Great Wall and another in 'Jesuit Baroque' style.

Many scholars believe that the fictional Daguan Yuan (Prospect Garden) of the classic Qing novel *Dream of the Red Chamber* was styled after Prince Gong's Mansion. John Minford, in his preface to the translation titled *The Story of the Stone*, notes that not only do the layouts correspond, but 'the architectural style and scale are so exactly what one would have expected, grand but in exquisite taste.'

That exquisite taste belonged to the first and most colourful of its owners, Heshen (1750–1799), who had risen from imperial bodyguard to grand councillor under the Qianlong emperor on the basis of his good looks and native wit. Qianlong was exceedingly (some whispered excessively) devoted to Heshen, even allowing him at the age of 27 to ride his horse within the Forbidden City. Heshen dipped so liberally into the public purse that he is considered possibly the most corrupt official in Chinese history – a title for which there's intense competition – though some scholars maintain the besotted emperor opened the purse himself.

In any case, when he built his garden mansion by Shichahai in 1776, he needed to build a two-storey brick building almost

200 m long with more than 40 rooms just to store his loot. His trove included 24 solid-gold beds inlaid with precious gems, 400 solid gold eating utensils, and 100,000 precious porcelain vessels. The total value of his property equalled ten years of Qing imperial revenue. Qianlong's successor, Jiaqing, was far less entranced. He charged Heshen with twenty crimes, about half of which related to acting above his station. Only the two highest ranks of Qing princes, those with the closest blood ties to the throne, were legally entitled to *wangfu*, a class to which Heshen's residence unashamedly aspired. He'd even had the audacity to build a hall there based on Qianlong's Forbidden City Palace of Tranquil Longevity.

Jiaqing had Heshen sentenced to death by a 'thousand cuts', but permitted him to commit suicide instead. In 1799 the court generously provided him with a gold-coloured silk ribbon. He lives on as a popular stock villain in television, film and stage shows about the Qing dynasty.

Part of the estate is called Wanfuyuan, the Garden of Ten Thousand Bats – bat, *fu*, 蝠, being a homonym for good fortune, *fu*, 福, and *wan*, ten thousand, being a highly propitious number in Chinese cosmology. This was a mystery, however, for there appeared to be only 9,999 representations of bats and the character 福 in the garden, including a bat-shaped

A Great Wall for the Princely Garden: Heshen's imperial ambitions.

The Jesuit Baroque gate in Prince Gong's Mansion.

pond. Other bats, and the character for 'good luck', were carved, drawn or fired into the garden's roof tiles, doorjambs, eaves and latticework.

Qianlong's grandfather, the great Kangxi emperor, had once famously written the character 福 in a large, fluid and elegant hand. The calligraphy was carved into a large stone that was believed to ensure anyone who touched it good

Another view of the baroque gateway, decorated for the Chinese New Year.

One of the mansion's many charming vistas, early spring 2014.

fortune. But the stone disappeared. After Heshen's death it was discovered hidden in a cave inside an artificial mount in the Garden of Ten Thousand Bats: it was the 10,000th *fu*. Jiaqing was furious. Because Heshen affixed the stone to the cave wall with stone-carved dragon heads, it was impossible to remove without breaking it. Believing that the talismanic power of the stone could allow Heshen's descendants to prosper despite his disgrace, Jiaqing ordered the cave sealed. Only in the Mao era, when Premier Zhou ordered the cave opened, was it rediscovered. Once the garden was opened to the public in the mid-1990s, Chinese tourists began rubbing it smooth; today it is under a pane of glass smudged by the palms of thousands of fortune-seeking visitors.

In 1852 the Xianfeng emperor granted the estate to his younger brother Prince Gong, also known as Yixin. That's when it properly joined the ranks of official Qing *wangfu*, princely mansions, of which there were about 90. (The Ming also had princely mansions – Wangfujing, the 'Well of the Princely Mansions', was named for the ten that once lined that street.)

The emperor charged Prince Gong with protecting the capital. When he fled the Allied troops in 1860, Prince

Gong conducted the negotiations with Lord Elgin and the French representative Baron Gros following the burning of the Yuanmingyuan that resulted in one of the most notorious 'unequal treaties' in Qing history at his Shichahai estate.

After Xianfeng's death, Prince Gong supported Cixi's bid for power. As prince-councillor, he capably guided reforms of China's military defences, transportation and communications networks and acted as China's first Foreign Minister. But his relationship with Cixi grew strained. She sacked him in the early 1870s when he opposed her proposal to rebuild the Yuanmingyuan, insisting that it was an unaffordable luxury. Taking refuge from politics in his estate, he devoted himself to poetry and entertaining.

Like most Manchu noblemen, Prince Gong adored the opera. But Qing noblemen were forbidden to frequent the theatres of the common people, so they built private theatres at home. Prince Gong's was particularly grand, set within a peony garden and housing his own troupe – the only one at the time that specialized in the ancient form known as *kunqu*, one of the forebears of Peking Opera. The troupe, which lasted only two years, consisted of some of the greatest singers of the time. Their disciples included several of *kunqu* and Peking Opera's greatest stars, including Mei Lanfang.

Well in the grounds of Prince Gong's Mansion with good-fortune cards bearing Kangxi's calligraphed *fu*.

In the midst of the disastrous Sino-Japanese War of 1894–5, Cixi recalled the elderly prince-councillor out of retirement. He died of illness three years later and the mansion passed to his descendants. When the Republicans overthrew the Qing in 1911–12, his descendants sold off parts of the estate and mortgaged others to fund a movement to restore the Qing as well as pay off personal debts. In 1937, Fu-Jen Catholic University moved their women's campus and school of fine arts onto its grounds.

After the Communists took control in 1949, the chiefs of the Public Security Bureau responsible for the protection of state leaders moved in, along with Soviet KGB agents and advisers. As a result, as Geremie Barmé has written, it 'effectively disappeared from the map of Beijing, becoming literally a "secret garden"'. Later, the Chinese Academy of Music and the Art and Literature Research Institute of the Ministry of Culture set up in another section of the expansive estate, coexisting there with the security personnel and a factory manufacturing air conditioners.

This was not unusual – even the Temple of Heaven ceded some 4 sq. km of grounds to shops, schools, factories and a radio station bristling with antennae. Central government offices occupy a considerable portion of the Forbidden City; the *China Heritage Quarterly* has reported that as late as 2004, of Beijing's 3,500 historical buildings, 60 per cent 'still accommodated legal "squatters"'. Over the years its tenants knocked down many of the garden's old buildings and erected new structures in its courtyards. Gardens that once rivalled those of the south have been neglected into decay and remaining antiques funnelled into private and public collections.

Less than two dozen princely mansions survive, in varying states of preservation, today. Banks, embassies and the Communist aristocracy occupy many of them. All are in the vicinity of Shichahai and Beihai Park. It is sobering to think that of all the ones that are open to the public today, Prince Gong's (rebuilt) Mansion, which bears the designation Princely Mansion Museum, is despite all that's been done to it still the best-preserved of all those open to the public.

The rooms from the Palace of Tranquil Longevity recreated by Heshen, remade again for show.

The last time I was there, I happened to arrive at the theatre in the peony garden just as it was letting in a mix of foreign and Chinese tourists for a show. There would be Peking Opera, I was told. Unlike most of my Beijing contemporaries and nearly all my younger Chinese friends, who can't abide it, I actually do love Peking Opera. I didn't have great expectations for the opera. But I did want to have a look at Prince Gong's celebrated theatre. Buying a ticket, I filed in to be seated at a table and served with sticky snacks and a cup of something that was to good Chinese tea what floor sweepings are to fresh herbs. I gritted my teeth throughout the first act, an accident-prone performance of juggling and acrobatics by what appeared to be very small children with extremely forced smiles. When the 'Peking Opera' performance turned out to involve the depiction of a flirtatious young woman by a prancing, badly made-up, middle-aged man with swinging jowls and the clumsiest hand gestures and worst singing I have ever heard on a Beijing stage – possibly any stage – I felt the end of civilization had come. As the plainly bored attendants herded out the benumbed audience, I lingered as long as possible to restore the sense that once, here, things had been different: as beautiful and as cultured as anywhere in this wide world.

Stacks of tea, Maliandao Tea Street.

LISTINGS

HOTELS

Aman at Summer Palace
No. 1 Gongmen Forward Street, Yiheyuan, Haidian district.
www.amanresorts.com/amanatsummerpalace/home.aspx

Live large like an emperor or empress in the Aman, close by the East Gate of Cixi's Summer Palace. Fabulous food, cocktails and atmosphere at imperial prices.

The Orchid Hotel
65 Baochao Hutong, Gulou East Street, Dongcheng district
www.theorchidbeijing.com

A small, beautiful, well-run and welcoming designer *hutong* hotel in the shadow of the Drum Tower.

Mao'er Courtyard
28 Mao'er Hutong, Dongcheng district. www.maoer28.com

This intimate converted family courtyard home is a much-awarded treasure for those on a budget wanting to experience *hutong* life. On a historic *hutong* linking Shichahai with Nanluoguxiang.

The Opposite House
Building 1, Taikoo Li Sanlitun North, 11 Sanlitun Road, Chaoyang district.
www.theoppositehouse.com

Chic, architect-designed boutique hotel just steps away from the Village at Sanlitun. Spot the celebrity.

Grace Beijing
No. 1, 706 Houjie, 798 Art District, No. 2 Jiuxianqiao, Chaoyang district.
www.gracehotels.com/beijing

The only hotel in the 798 art zone, a luxury boutique hotel on the site of a nineteenth-century crystal factory. The decor is a mix of Chinese tradition and modernity.

MUSEUMS

The Forbidden City (Palace Museum)
Entry through the Meridian Gate (accessible via Tiananmen or Donghuamen on the palace's eastern flank). www.dpm.org.cn

The home of emperors and empresses from the fourteenth century through to the early twentieth, its architecture is the greatest treasure on daily display today. Best visited off-season to avoid what can be crushing crowds. Imperial treasures, from textiles to rare calligraphic scrolls, are featured in changing exhibitions above the Meridian Gate and in the Hall of Martial Valour (Wuying Dian) in the southwest sector of the palace – the side corridors are also well worth exploring. A Beijing must-see.

Beijing Urban Planning Exhibition Hall
20 Qianmen East Street, Chongwen district. www.bjghzl.com.cn

This superb museum on the southeast corner of Tiananmen Square tells the story of Beijing itself with clever, multi-media exhibits that include models illustrating how the graceful ceramic roofs and eaves of Beijing's courtyard dwellings are constructed, a 3-D scale floor map of the city, an introduction to the most famous artisans and guilds of the Qing dynasty, and much more. Highly recommended.

Beijing Capital Museum
16 Fuxingmenwai Dajie, West City. www.capitalmuseum.org.cn

This newish museum at the west end of Chang'an Avenue features interactive, multilingual and multimedia exhibitions on Beijing history, court life, folk customs and art. There's a floor on *hutong* life and a level devoted to Peking Opera, with a recreated theatre and a valuable collection of Mei Lanfang's original costumes and scripts.

National Art Museum of China
1 Wusi Dajie, East City, just northeast of the Palace Museum. www.namoc.org

Built in 1958 and renovated in 2005, this enormous museum has some art from the Ming, Qing and Republican periods, but its focus is on the post-1949 era. Its exhibitions have ranged from Salvador Dalí to contemporary Chinese art and artists. Although it tends towards relatively staid fare these days, as the China Art Gallery it hosted the first major exhibition of China's 'unofficial' art collective, the Stars, in 1980, and the wildest postmodernist exhibition in China's history, 'No U-Turn', in 1989.

Police Museum
36 Dongjiaominxiang Lane, Dongcheng district

Housed in the former Citibank Building in the old Legation Quarter, this fascinating museum offers an insight into Beijing crime and punishment through the ages. Displays include policemen's whistles, badges and uniforms from different time periods, a Cultural Revolution-era wheel-shaped filing cabinet for local residential permits, guns that have belonged to various Communist leaders, and the formerly top-secret map of Kim Il-sung's 1987 Beijing tour.

Gongwangfu
17 Qianhai West Street, West City. www.pgm.org.cn

On a *hutong* that runs off the Back Lake of Shichahai, the Mansion of Prince Gong, or the Princely Mansion Museum, as it is now called, is the best-preserved residence of a noble family in Beijing that is open to the public – and its story is a microcosm of the last several hundred years of Beijing history (see pp. 231–7).

Guanfu Museum
18 Jinnan Road, Zhangwangfeng, Dashanzi, Chaoyang district. www.guanfumuseum.org.cn (in Chinese)

The first private art museum in China holds the extraordinary collection of the autodidact antiquities scholar and television personality Ma Weidu. Standouts in this intimate, well-designed museum not far from the 798 art district are the ceramics and furniture, including a fabulous assembly of traditional doors and windows.

Former Residence of Lao She
19 Fengfu Lane, West Dengshikou Street, East City

This is the home lived in by the iconic Beijing writer Lao She and his family from 1949 until he died as a result of persecution in the Cultural Revolution. The calendar on the desk is left open to the date of his death, and on his bed, cards are laid out in a half-finished game of solitaire.

Former Residence of Mei Lanfang
9 Huguosi Street, West City

Once part of a major princely residence, this is where China's most revered star of Peking Opera, Mei Lanfang, lived after 1950. It screens footage of his performances and features a pictorial display of his most famous poses and hand movements as well as a great collection of scripts and so on, donated by family members.

Museum of the War of Chinese People's Resistance Against Japanese Aggression, Wanping
101 Chengnei Jie, Marco Polo Bridge, Fengtai district.
www.1937china.com/enweb

The most comprehensive museum in China on the subject of the eight-year Japanese occupation and Chinese resistance is well worth the trip to the city's southwest. Its exhibits of weaponry, uniforms, photographs and propaganda materials from both sides as well as from the Japanese push into Asia generally are riveting, especially if you're a history buff. It's located inside the Ming-era fortress town of Wanping, in Fengtai district. On your way out, look for the Japanese mortar holes in Wanping's walls. Marco Polo Bridge is on Wanping's doorstep and the Peking Man World Heritage Site at Zhoukoudian is not too far a drive away.

SITES

Great Walls

The classic views of Badaling – a model of reconstruction in the style of the Ming Great Walls – attract the masses, but you might want to check out the walls at Mutianyu or other less-trammelled sectors such as steep Juyongguan. If you're adventurous, fit and equipped for hiking, try the fragmented, unreconstructed and often breathtakingly scenic 'wild Great Walls' scattered throughout the mountains around Beijing.

Tiananmen Square
Dongcheng district

The largest public square in the world, expanded to its current size in the late 1950s, has been the site of historical demonstrations, dramas and spectacles from the anti-imperialist demonstrations of 4 May 1919 to the Red Guard rallies of the 1960s, the student-led pro-democracy protests of 1989 that culminated in massacre, and the grand parades staged in celebration of such events as the 60th anniversary of the nation's founding in 2009. Tiananmen Square is the site of the Monument to the People's Heroes and Mao Zedong's Mausoleum.

Dashila'r
Southwest of Tiananmen Square

The narrow, old and winding *hutong* that still remain in this historic yet development-endangered neighbourhood that was once part of the Ming and Qing dynasty's Outer City are as close as you'll come today to the Republican era Beijing of Lao She's early novels. As the bulldozers roll over Dashila'r, the area's remaining old brothels, teahouses and temples have drawn hipsters, baristas and fashionistas to set up shop here – pop-up and stay-put alike. Full of surprises.

Temple of Heaven (Tiantan)
Enter by any of four gates (north, south, east, west); the east gate is on the No. 5 subway line. www.tiantanpark.com/cn

Literally the 'Altar of Heaven', this is the site where generations of emperors enacted elaborate rituals to pray for good harvests. Its symbolically rich layout and unique architecture are set within an expansive park where locals exercise, sing, play chess and hold matchmaking events to find marriage partners for their children.

Lama Temple (Yonghegong)
12 Yonghegong Dajie, Dongcheng district

At one time a princely mansion and home to the young prince who would become the Yongzheng emperor, the Lama Temple is the only temple in the city that is roofed with the golden tiles that denote an imperial palace. It is the largest and best-preserved Tibetan Buddhist temple in Beijing.

Yuanmingyuan (Old Summer Palace)
Park entrance at 28 Qinghua West Road, Haidian district; on the No. 4 subway line

The eighteenth-century garden palace, the name of which translates as the Garden of Perfect Brightness, once represented the pinnacle of the aesthetic achievement of three Manchu emperors. In 1860 British and French troops punitively looted and burned its legendary buildings to the ground. The elegiac ruins of the Yuanmingyuan have been a magnet for poets and patriots ever since. Like the Summer Palace nearby, the Yuanmingyuan is no longer in Beijing's rural outskirts but part of the megalopolis, even meriting its own subway station.

Summer Palace (Yiheyuan)
Haidian district; one stop after the Yuanmingyuan on the No. 4 subway line

On the shores of the Yuan dynasty reservoir of Kunming Lake stand the scattered pavilions, temples and walkways of the Yiheyuan, the preferred residence of the Empress Dowager Cixi in her later years. Among its attractions are the infamous marble boat, a long covered walkway that follows the course of the lake, and the hilltop Tower of Buddhist Incense.

Beihai Park and Shichahai
By Di'anmen, northwest of the Forbidden City

The linked waterways of Shichahai and Beihai are among the greatest delights of old Beijing. Stroll, or pedal a boat in summer, skate or sled in winter, and drop in on Prince Gong's Mansion while you're there; if you have a taste for amplified pop music, stay on for happy hour. Shop for souvenirs on Yandai Xiejie (Tobacco Pipe Slanted Street), take a *hutong* tour by pedicab. Just don't jump in the water. To the west, northwest and southwest of the Drum and Bell Towers, the lakes are in Xicheng district.

Western Hills

Beijing people love to visit the Western Hills in the autumn, when the changing colours of the leaves on the trees make the vistas a riot of colour. But the relative freshness of the mountain air and the area's many temples, including the magnificent Biyun Si (Temple of the Azure Clouds) and Wofo Si (Temple of the Reclining Buddha) on the grounds of the Beijing Botanical Garden make heading for the hills an especially attractive idea in spring and summer as well.

Peking Man World Heritage Site
Zhoukoudian Village, Fangshan County

The best thing you can say about the tacky statues littered about the place of Peking Man, Peking Woman, the sabre-tooth cats and other predators, and the deer that appear to be on the menu of all the above, are that they've passed into the realm of amusing kitsch. The museum, forced to display replica bones and skulls until the real Peking Man finally decides to call home (see chapter One), is a trifle underwhelming. You can't get into all the caves. But this is it. It's where it all began, or at least one of the places where it all began. Not just Beijing. Humanity. Awesome in the original sense of the word. And the view is magnificent.

ENTERTAINMENT VENUES

National Centre for the Performing Arts
2 West Chang'an Street, Xicheng district. www.chncpa.org

The titanium and glass dome to one side of Tiananmen Square, known officially as the 'Pearl on Water' and unofficially as the 'Egg in Albumen', presents concerts, operas, plays and other performances from around China and the world in four well-designed, purpose-built theatres.

Mei Lanfang Grand Theatre
32 Ping'anlixi Dajie, Xicheng district

The home of the National Peking Opera Company (NPOC), this fan-shaped theatre was named for the most famous actor of the Peking Opera and former president of the NPOC. It hosts other shows as well, but whatever you're seeing, don't forget to check out the display of Peking Opera costumes on the second floor. English-language listings for the Mei Lanfang as well as other theatres, including the popular Poly as well as the Workers Stadium, can be found at www.theatrebeijing.com.

Workers Stadium
Workers Stadium North Road

Built in 1959 as one of Mao's 'Ten Great Structures' and renovated in 2004, the stadium's colourful history includes hosting the PRC's first National Sports Meet, violent Red Guard 'struggle sessions' and China's first local and international rock concerts. With a capacity of 80,000, today it presents a variety of sports, musical and other events.

Yugong Yishan
3–2 Zhangzizhong Lu, Dongcheng district. www.yugongyishan.com

Named for the Maoist parable 'The Foolish Old Man Moves the Mountain', this venue pulls the biggest local and international rock acts; it also puts on film nights and DJs. Rock fans will also want to check out **Mao Livehouse**, a warehouse-style rock venue near the Drum Tower, also featuring local and foreign acts (111 Gulou Dongdajie, Dongcheng district).

East Shore Live Jazz Café (Dong An)
2 Qianhai South Shore, 2f, Di'anmenwai Dajie, West City

Kick back and groove to jazz on the shores of Shichahai at Qianhai. Owner Liu Yuan is the legendary saxophonist from the band of China's first rocker, Cui Jian; this is a place where musicians hang out. The views of Shichahai's Front Lake (Qianhai) are wonderful. If you prefer the blues, check out **Café CD Blues**, owned by bassist Zhang Ling, another former band-mate of Cui Jian (39 Shen Lu Jie, 1–28 Ritan Upper Street, Chaoyang district. www.cdblues.cn).

Lao She Teahouse
Building 3, Zhengyang Market, Qianmen West Street, West City. www.laosheteahouse.net

Named for one of the most famous plays by celebrated Beijing writer Lao She, this reconstructed, cleaned-up version of an old Qianmen teahouse offers meals, snacks and bite-size performances that may include Chinese opera, comedy cross-talk and acrobatics for an audience of mainly tourists and Chinese out-of-towners. Nightly shows at 7:50 p.m.

UME Huaxing International Cineplex
No. 44 Kexueyuan South Road, Shuangyushu, Haidian district.
www.bjume.com (in Chinese)

Beijing's first five-star Cineplex. **Megabox** at Sanlitun's Village
is also a good place to catch both Western and Chinese films
(b1/f Sanlitun Village South, 19 Sanlitun Lu, Chaoyang district).
English-language listings at www.taikoolisanlitun.com/eng.

Chaoyang Theatre
36 North East Third Ring Road, Chaoyang district. www.chaoyangtheatre.com

The nightly acrobatic shows are flashier and on a bigger stage at the
Chaoyang but if you want to see acrobats in the neighbourhood
where once you could watch them on the street, try those at the
Tianqiao Acrobatic Theatre (95 Tianqiao Shichang Lu, east end
of Beiwei Lu, Xuanwu district, opposite the Tianqiao Theatre.
www.tianqiaoacrobatictheater.com).

Forbidden City Concert Hall
West Chang'an Avenue, Zhongshan Park, Xicheng district. www.fcchbj.com
(in Chinese)

One of Beijing's largest and best concert halls, set in historic
Zhongshan Park, just west of Tiananmen. Traditional, classical
and chamber music are the staples of this 1,400-seat theatre with
its excellent acoustics and charming historical surrounds.

Red Theatre
Near the Temple of Heaven, at 44 Xingfu Dajie, Chongwen district.
www.redtheatre.cn

Shaolin kung fu via Vegas. Over-the-top spectacle with a touch of Zen.

RESTAURANTS

Manfulou
38 Di'anmennei Dajie, Xicheng district

This Mongolian hotpot restaurant is a reliable, atmospheric and
reasonably priced *lao zihao*, or 'old brand' restaurant. Just north

of Jingshan Park, close to Shichahai, it serves Beijing's favourite cold-weather meal: frozen sliced lamb and other meats, vegetables, tofu and vermicelli that you cook in individual hotpots and eat with accompaniments such as sesame buns and pickled garlic.

Da Dong Roast Duck
1–2f, Nanxincang International Plaza, 22a Dongsishitiao, Dongcheng.
www.dadongdadong.com/en

Quanjude is *the* iconic Peking duck restaurant with branches throughout the city, including one at 30 Qianmen Street that is the largest Peking duck restaurant in the world. I prefer others – check various websites for the duck restaurant du jour. Da Dong at the old Imperial Granary Nanxincang offers lean duck and other dishes such as sautéed chestnuts with Chinese cabbage and stewed veal with wild mushrooms, in an upmarket atmosphere with friendly service. Desserts include double-boiled lily bulbs with rose jelly and tiramisu with toffee fruit.

Old Beijing Zhajiang Noodle King
56 Dongxinglong Street, Chongwen district

This unpretentious, noisy, cheap and cheerful restaurant north of the Temple of Heaven specializes in hand-pulled noodles and traditional, tasty Beijing fare. The signature dish, *zhajiang mian*, is a hearty bowl of noodles with stir-fried minced pork, fresh vegetables and savoury fermented soybean paste.

Baoyuan Jiaozi Wu
6 Maizidian Jie, Chaoyang district

Baoyuan Jiaozi Wu serves a rainbow variety of (naturally coloured) dumplings with a range of fillings and accompaniments. The decor is as colourful as the dumplings. Vegetarian options include crackling rice-filled purple dumplings and lotus root dumplings in a spinach-green skin. But Beijing is full of great dumpling restaurants. Check online listings for up-to-date recommendations.

Imperial Cuisine
Various locations

Once, **Fangshan Tang**, on the north shore of Hortensia Island, inside an imperial pavilion with a fabulous view onto Beihai Park (www.fangshanfanzhuang.com.cn), was a de rigueur Beijing experience. Today the view remains spectacular; the food not so much. A second well-known imperial banquet restaurant is located in another scenic and historic building, one of Empress Dowager Cixi's opera theatres and banquet halls in the Summer Palace: **Tingliguan**. Tingliguan (the Pavilion for Listening to the Orioles Restaurant), on the south slope of Longevity Hill in the Summer Palace, by Kunming Lake, does three lunch sittings during the high tourist season. But if you want the full Qing extravaganza (costumed servers, music and so on) done in style and with better food, then head to the **Bai Family Garden Restaurant**, situated on the grounds of a former princely mansion at 15 Suzhou St, Haidian. Or, for a more intimate experience, go to the also well-reviewed, tiny but lovely **Li Family Restaurant** near the Back Lake and the old Deshengmen city gate: 11 Yangfang Hutong, Denei Avenue. The grandfather of the owner, maths professor Li Shanlin, was Minister of Household Affairs for the Qing court. Reservations are necessary for both the Bai and Li family restaurants.

Zhong Ba Lou (Middle 8)
8 Dongsanlitun Zhong Jie, Chaoyang district (opposite the 3.3 Shopping Centre in the Sanlitun bar street)

The spicy, piquant tastes of China's southwest, including Sichuan, Guizhou and Yunnan, are popular in Beijing. This Yunnan eatery offers everything from succulent banana leaf-wrapped meats to insects for the adventurous. Chic, clean, popular. Not cheap, but not over-priced.

Gui Jie (Ghost Street)
Dongzhimennei Dajie, Dongcheng district

A street of noisy, popular restaurants that comes alive at night – every night, all night. Strings of red lanterns and lines of double-parked cars tell you you've arrived. Follow the crowds to the popular places:

you'll find everything here from spicy Sichuanese to hotpot, seafood and vegetarian. The shouting you hear is the sound of Chinese drinking games. Ghost Street is where serious drinkers come to eat. The *gui* in the original name signified an old-style food container; people switched to the homonym meaning 'ghost' when street food vendors set up in the pre-dawn hours in the 1990s to feed taxi drivers and shift workers, their lanterns and dim lights creating a 'ghostly' atmosphere. Stalls gave way to restaurants, but the all-night tradition – and the lanterns – remain.

1949 – The Hidden City
Behind Pacific Century Place on Gongti Beilu (Workers Stadium North Road) in Sanlitun, Chaoyang district

An upmarket cluster of restaurants, bars, art and events spaces, and even a noodle bar, in what *City Weekend* describes as '6,000 sq. meters of neo-industrial chic' – the former Beijing Machinery and Electric Institute. Duck de Chine serves Peking duck and confit de canard, Bollie optional. One of a number of dining complexes in the city.

Kong Yiji
2a Dongming Hutong Deshengmennei Dajie, Houhai (Back Lake), Xicheng district

This charming and atmospheric, reasonably priced restaurant next to Shichahai's Back Lake features southern Zhejiang cuisine. Its 'stinky beancurd' (*chou doufu*) and stewed fatty pork (*dongpo rou*) are sublime, and there's plenty on the menu for less adventurous palates in this lovely old restaurant. The paths to the front door are lined with ceramic wine pots. A personal favourite.

Capital M
3f, No. 2 Qianmen Pedestrian Street (just south of Tiananmen Square). www.capital-m-beijing.com

First-rate Western food in a stylish restaurant-cum-bar on the eastern side of Qianmen Shopping Street, this Australian-run restaurant has a to-die-for view of the old city gates all the way (on a clear day) to Tiananmen and beyond. Capital M also runs a yearly literary festival with international guests and hosts other cultural events such as chamber music concerts; check the website for details.

BARS AND CAFÉS

Flat White
Various locations. www.caffelaffare.com.cn

New Zealanders are behind this excellent café mini-chain and the Rickshaw Roasters that is its home brew. Flat White has branches in 798, the Silk Market, the embassy district of Dongzhimen and elsewhere.

Backyard
Liangmahe Nanlu, Chaoyang district

Located on the south side of the Liangma River in Sanlitun, the pocket-sized Backyard serves Rickshaw Roasters coffee, free-range eggs and healthy, creative dishes with vegetarian options and home-made bread. Detox by day, return at night for a glass of wine. Other notable cafés on the riverbank include a branch of Wudaoying's popular Vineyard Café (see below).

Wudaoying Hutong and Environs
Close to the Lama Temple and both Andingmen and Yonghegong subway stations

This *hutong* close to the Lama Temple and other *hutong* in the vicinity are packed with interesting small bars, cafés and shops. The Vineyard Café (31 Wudaoying Hutong), with its skylit courtyard, weekend brunch and Tuesday–Friday lunch deals, is a stalwart of the scene; its seedling Vine Leaf (9 Jianchang Hutong) picks up the slack on Monday. Vegetarians praise the hummus at the vegan café Veggie Table, open from 11 a.m. to 11 p.m. Some venues present live music at night, including jazz.

Gu Lou (The Drum Tower)
The neighbourhood on all sides of the Drum Tower

The streets and *hutong* around the Drum and Bell Towers, including Nanluoguxiang, have seen bars and cafés come and go; at the time of publication, the shabby-hip Temple in the complex at 206 Gulou Dong Dajie was on the hot list, but the heat goes out of places pretty quickly in Beijing, so best to check current listings.

Bookworm

4 Nan Sanlitun Road, Chaoyang district. www.beijingbookworm.com

A café within a cosy, vibrant English-language bookshop and reading library that features a regular programme of English-language activities, including author talks and its own writers' festival.

Chocolate

Northwest corner of Ritan Park

A vast, literally underground Russian nightclub featuring live entertainment and, according to *City Weekend*, 'half of Vladivostok'. Smoke hookahs, drink flaming cocktails, admire yourself in gilded mirrors by the light of chandeliers and relieve yourself in golden toilets. Chocolate is best consumed before midnight.

Workers Stadium and Bar Street

Gongti (Workers Stadium) Beilu and Sanlitun Beilu

Pumping nightclubs, bars and beer barns of varying degrees of salubriousness cluster in and around these Sanlitun landmarks. Mix it up with clubbers of all nations, nouveau riche Chinese businessmen, desperados and Chinese 'models', 'actresses' and other faux-ingénues on the make. Money might just buy you love.

Destination

Dong Yingfanghutong, 7 Gongti (Workers Stadium) West Road, Chaoyang district. www.bjdestinaton.com

DJs, cultural activities, free HIV testing and the odd art exhibition make this multi-level warren of bars and lounges more than just Beijing's premier gay bar. The cruise ship picks up steam after 10 p.m.; Wednesdays and weekends is when things really kick off.

Timezone 8

4 Jiuxianqiao Lu, Dashanzi Art District, Chaoyang district (across from Ullens Center in 798). www.timezone8.com

This café-restaurant-bar in the heart of the 798 art district is associated with an art and design bookshop. For top places to eat in 798 check online listings.

Element Fresh
Various locations. www.elementfresh.com

Element Fresh calls itself a restaurant, and it's bigger than any other café, but its consistently good coffees and seasonal café-style meals (including sandwiches, pasta and a superb range of salads) let it squeeze on to this list. The one in Sanlitun Village features an outdoor seating area that is delightful when the weather is too.

SHOPS

Panjiayuan
Third Ring Road East, Chaoyang district

The days when a careful search could turn up a priceless heirloom – or even an authentic Little Red Book – may have passed, but this bustling, historic flea market bazaar still tantalizes with the promise that somewhere amid the new-for-old Tang porcelains and born-yesterday Mao badges there may lie true gems. One Beijing native's trash . . .

Silk Markets
8 Xiushui East Street, Chaoyang district. www.silkstreet.cc (in Chinese)

Replacing a thriving laneway of street stalls selling knock-off designer fashions, the Silk Markets is a clamorous multi-storey clothing bazaar on Xiushui Jie ('Silk Street'). The old Qing dynasty name for the place was *choushui*, 'stinky water'. There are plenty of other such markets and a number of similar places, some with more reliable designer brands and less clamour, but the Silk Markets is your Daddy. Bargain hard here.

Liulichang
Liulichang Xijie, Xuanwu district. www.ebeijing.gov.cn/feature_2/liulichang

After the Yuan dynasty established its imperial kiln in Haiwang Village, it was renamed Liulichang, Glazed Tile Factory; the kilns produced the golden roof tiles and other ceramic tiles for both the Yuan and Ming palaces. By the eighteenth century the area was famed for its antique shops, and in the early twentieth century hosted a lively and progressive publishing scene. Rebuilt as a replica of its former self in the early 1980s, nearly a kilometre of shops along Liulichang Street specialize in scrolls, paintings, seal carvings and the traditional 'four treasures of the study': brush, ink stick, ink stone and paper.

Yandai Xiejie (Tobacco Pipe Slanting Street)
Very close to Shichahai's Back Lake, Di'anmen, Xicheng

Every souvenir you could possibly want to snare, from folding lanterns and teapots to panda-head hats and Mao-branded teacups and other kitsch is on sale here, along with such seasonal necessities as rabbit-fur earmuffs for winter, fans for summer and Tibetan jewellery for all occasions. This still-atmospheric street, crooked like a pipe, leads to the lakes of Shichahai.

798 Art District
4 Jiuxianqiao Road, Chaoyang district

The Bauhaus-designed former military-industrial complex turns out art, design and fashion – some of it quite exceptional – the way it used to turn out rocket components. Buy art, clothes, design.

Xinjiekou South Street
Xinjiekou Nanjie, Xicheng

This street is packed with shops selling both Western and Chinese traditional musical instruments, sheet music and CDs. Many of the shops offer music lessons as well. Haggling over price is acceptable in many of these shops, but beware of counterfeit Western brands, especially with such things as electric guitars. If you've mastered your instrument, the street also boasts a number of recording studios, including some where China's top rock and other musicians have made their most iconic albums.

The Village
Stretching over several blocks, it is most easily accessed via Gongti Beilu or Sanlitun Beijie. www.sanlitunvillage.com

Come here for brands, local as well as international, not bargaining. Clothing (from agnès b. to Ziggy Chen), Apple products, imported foodstuffs, homewares – The Village has it all. Shop till you need to drop into one of this pleasant, multi-structure shopping centre's many restaurants, cafés, bars or even its multiplex cinema. Be sure to stop in on the local designers' showcase Brand New China at NLG-09A, Sanlitun Village North.

Bookshops

The **Beijing Books Building** is a Xidan district landmark: floor after dizzying floor of books, audio-visual and other related products (17 West Chang'an Avenue, Xicheng. www.bjbb.com, in Chinese). If you're looking for English-language books, however, best head to **Chaterhouse Booktrader** (B107 The Place, 9 Guanghua Lu, CBD/Guomao), **Bookworm** (Sanlitun Nanjie, Bldg 4), with its programme of events and reading library (see listing under Bars and Cafés), or one of the several branches of the Singapore chain **Page One**, whose Sanlitun branch, along with its café, is open 24/7 (1–2f, Building s2, The Village. www.pageonegroup.com/1/china.html).

Tea Street
11 Maliandao Road, Xuanwu District

Over 1,000 tea shops cluster here, inside a four-storey building where wholesale dealers sell brews from everywhere in China, and in the many shops that spill down the side streets as well. Buy tea, teapots and accessories – even tea tables – in Beijing's largest tea mart and north China's biggest tea distribution centre.

Eyeglasses City
East Third Ring Road Nan Lu (South Road), near the Jinsong subway station, Chaoyang district

Just as once there were guild streets specializing in jade polishing or palace headgear, you can now find clusters of like shops selling electronics, guitars and – a personal favourite – eyeglasses. At this cluster of optometrist shops, they'll test your eyes, help you choose your frames and then send you off for a coffee while they grind the lenses: the whole process takes about an hour for straightforward prescriptions.

CHRONOLOGY

780,000–100,000 years ago
Peking Man and other hominids inhabit caves in Fangshan county in what is now southwest Beijing.

7th century BCE
A small walled town called Ji in what today is the southwestern sector of Beijing's Inner City becomes part of the city-state of Yan and flourishes. Over the centuries, the city is conquered, assimilated and renamed (Yan, Youzhou) numerous times.

283–209 BCE
Defensive 'Great Walls' of tamped earth crest the ridges of the mountains north of the city.

938 CE
The Buddhist Khitans conquer the city, make it the secondary capital of the Liao dynasty, and rename it Nanjing and later Yanjing.

1115
The Jurchens, ancestors of the Manchus, establish the Jin dynasty; in 1553, having vanquished the Liao, they move their capital to Yanjing and rename it Zhongdu.

1179
The Jin Shizong emperor constructs Hortensia Isle in Taiye Pond, today's Beihai Park.

1214

Genghis Khan 'knocks on the gates' of the city, and leaves with hostages and plunder. He visits again a year later and inflicts 'glorious slaughter'.

1271

Genghis's grandson Khubilai Khan makes the city the capital of the Yuan dynasty and Mongol-ruled China. He will give the city, renamed Khanbalik, its grid-like layout and first *hutong* laneways. Later, Marco Polo visits and calls it one of the world's grandest cities.

1368

Founding of the Ming dynasty. The Ming becomes the fourth dynasty and in 1421 the first Han Chinese one to make the city its capital, renaming it Beijing. The Ming palace precinct, including the Forbidden City, as well as the city walls and layout, including a new walled Outer City attached to the south wall of what is now called the Inner City, survive nearly intact until the Communist era.

1644

Li Zicheng's peasant army besieges Beijing. The Chongzhen emperor hangs himself on the artificial hill to the north of the palace, today's Jingshan Park. A Manchu army unseats the rebels and establishes Beijing as the capital of the Manchu Qing dynasty.

1648

The Qing court orders all ethnic Han Chinese, except those in the Manchu social, military and political organization known as the Banners, to leave the Inner City.

1790

The Qianlong emperor's 80th birthday celebration sees the birth of Peking Opera.

1860

Following the Second Opium War, the British dispatch a delegation to Beijing to demand greater concessions from the Qing court.

The emissaries are imprisoned and tortured in the magnificent imperial garden palace, the Yuanmingyuan. British and French forces march on Beijing and loot and burn the palace.

1861

The Xianfeng emperor dies. The Empress Dowager Cixi, acting as co-regent for her son, the young Tongzhi emperor, begins her rise to become one of nineteenth-century China's most powerful and controversial figures.

1900

A violently xenophobic and superstitious sect known as the Boxers, with the help of imperial forces, besieges the Legation Quarter for 55 days. Foreign troops invade the city to relieve the siege; they then loot and plunder. Cixi, the emperor and the court flee to the countryside.

November 1908

The Empress Dowager Cixi and her nephew, the Guangxu emperor, die, suspiciously, over a mere two-day period. The Xuantong emperor, three-year-old Puyi, becomes the last emperor to be enthroned in the Forbidden City.

1911

Republican revolution breaks out in the south of China.

1912

The new Republican government transfers to the north at the insistence of President Yuan Shikai. It's legal again for Chinese to reside in the Inner City.

1915

Yuan dissolves parliament and declares himself emperor; he dies the following year.

1917

The beginning of the Warlord Era, in which provincial military bosses conquer and loot Beijing in turn.

4 May 1919

Thousands of Peking University students march in protest at government concessions at foreign powers; this sparks a cultural and intellectual ferment known as the May Fourth Movement.

1924

Warlord Feng Yuxiang kicks Puyi out of the palace, which one year later opens some of its buildings and collection to the public as the Palace Museum.

8 July 1937

The Japanese instigate an incident at Marco Polo Bridge as a pretext for invading Beijing and the rest of China. They make Beijing the capital of their provisional government before moving it south in 1940, after the Rape of Nanjing.

1945

The Japanese surrender.

1949

Following years of civil war, the Communist army led by Mao Zedong 'peacefully liberates' Beijing. On 1 October Mao announces the founding of the People's Republic of China from Tiananmen.

1952

The demolition of Beijing's city walls and *pailou* begins.

1959

The 'Ten Great Structures' are erected for the tenth anniversary of the People's Republic. Tiananmen Square is expanded to its current size.

1966–76

The Cultural Revolution: million-strong Red Guard rallies in Tiananmen Square, wilful destruction of much of Beijing's physical heritage and violent factional battles on the streets and campuses.

1976

The Tiananmen Incident, Mao's death and the arrest of the 'Gang of Four'.

1978–9

Democracy Wall, and the launch of new leader Deng Xiaoping's Reform Era.

1989

Student protests against corruption and for democracy and occupation of Tiananmen Square end with Deng Xiaoping ordering the army to clear the streets and square. Approximately 1,000 are left dead, and untold numbers are wounded in the massacre of 3–4 June.

1992

The beginning of the real estate boom and the razing of historical neighbourhoods and *hutong*.

2008

Beijing Olympic Games.

2009

The pro-democracy activist Liu Xiaobo is sentenced to eleven years for subversion; he is awarded the Nobel Peace Prize the following year while still in prison.

2014

Beijing now has 21.2 million residents, six ring roads and seventeen subway lines, including one servicing the airport. Scientists liken effects of Beijing's air pollution to 'nuclear winter'; a video entitled 'Happy in Beijing', filmed on one of the capital's most polluted days and uploaded to Youku, goes viral.

References

p. 21 'The language of Beijing . . .'. Liu Yong et al., *Beijing lishi wenhua shiwu jiang* (*Fifteen Lectures on Beijing History and Culture*) (Beijing, 2009), p. 407.

p. 35 'The Daoists tell the story . . .'. The translation of the exchange is by Arthur Waley, in *Three Ways of Thought in Ancient China* (New York, 1956), pp. 13–14.

p. 42 'According to the linguist Zhang Qingchang . . .'. Zhang Qingchang, *Hutong yu qita* (*Hutong and Other Topics*) (Beijing, 1990), pp. 57–67.

p. 42 'The streets are so straight and wide . . .'. The translations from Marco Polo come from a number of sources, including 'More excerpts from *The Book of Sir Marco Polo: The Venetian* . . . , Chapters LXXVI and LXXVII: Description of the Great City of Kinsay, Which is the LXXVII of the Whole Country of Manzi', at http://afe.easia.columbia.edu/special/marco_polo.htm (accessed 23 January 2014), and Yule Cordier, *The Book of Ser Marco Polo, Cathay and the Way Thither*, as quoted in Juliet Bredon, *Peking* (Shanghai, 1919), p. 148.

p. 43 'The Grand Khan receives news . . .'. Odoric de Pordenone, quoted in René Grousset, *The Rise and Splendour of the Chinese Empire* (Berkeley and Los Angeles, CA, 1968), p. 254.

p. 47 'Marco Polo tells us that . . .'. See Marco Polo, 'The Fashion of the Great Kaan's Table at His High Feasts', in *The Travels of Marco Polo*, at http://ebooks.adelaide.edu.au, 10 November 2012.

p. 48 'The finest that I have ever seen . . .'. Pordenone, quoted in Grousset, *Rise and Splendour*, p. 253.

pp. 62–3 'Making the case for Beijing . . .'. For a complete account, see Kathlyn Liscombe, '"The Eight Views of Beijing": Politics in Literati Art', *Artibus Asiae,* XLIX/1–2 (1988–9), pp. 127–52.

p. 63 'As the capital of a Chinese dynasty . . .'. See Liu Yong et al., *Beijing lishi wenhua shiwu jiang*, p. 400.

p. 66 'At the time, a palace cook's monthly salary . . .'. Beijing Daxue Lishixi (Peking University History Department), *Beijing shi (Beijing History)* (Beijing, 2003), p. 173.

p. 66 'The best policing efforts of the Imperial Brocaded Guards . . .'. Ibid., p. 180.

p. 69 'The righteous saw moral corruption everywhere . . .'. Timothy Brook, *The Confusions of Pleasure: Commerce and Culture in Ming China* (Berkeley, CA, 1998), p. 73.

p. 69 'Wanli responded that such cruel punishments . . .'. Translated in Jasper Becker, *City of Heavenly Tranquility* (Oxford and New York, 2008), p. 56.

p. 70 'The king has ordered [General] Nan-zhong . . .'. Poem adapted and excerpted from Arthur Waley's translation of *The Book of Songs* by Claire Roberts, in Claire Roberts and Geremie R. Barmé, *The Great Wall of China* (Sydney, 2006), p. 16.

p. 70 'The great early twentieth-century writer . . .'. The translation of Lu Xun is from Geremie Barmé and John Minford, eds, *Seeds of Fire: Chinese Voices of Conscience* (New York, 1989), p. 1.

p. 70 'The narrator of the popular . . .'. The translation of the *River Elegy* narration is taken from Geremie Barmé and Linda Jaivin, eds, *New Ghosts, Old Dreams: Chinese Rebel Voices* (New York, 1992), p. 151.

p. 73 'Its population was "*gente effeminate*" . . .'. Jonathan D. Spence has written extensively about Ricci's experiences in Beijing in *The Memory Palace of Matteo Ricci* (New York, 1984); these examples are drawn from pp. 217–21.

p. 73 'A ruthless peasant rebel . . .'. See Stephen G. Haw, *Beijing: A Concise History* (New York, 2007), p. 64. Official histories tend to gloss over Li's record of murderous violence.

p. 78 'Should there come [into the neighbourhood] an outsider . . .'. The original reads '*yuyou wailai zhi ren, wu xiangjiu laili*'. See Beijing Daxue Lishixi, *Beijing shi*, p. 275.

p. 78 'Red-capped watchmen . . .'. The Kangxi emperor, translated in Jonathan Spence, *Emperor of China: Self-portrait of K'ang-Hsi* (New York, 1975), p. 63.

p. 81 'Among the patrons of the Dashila'r wine shops . . .'. The description of Li Yu comes from Liu Dongli, *Beijingde hongchen jiumeng* (*The Mortal Pleasures of Old Beijing*) (Beijing, 2009), pp. 51–7.

p. 84 'Believing that the expensive magnifying glass . . .'. See Chris Elder, *Old Peking: City of the Ruler of the World* (Hong Kong, 1997), p. 62.

p. 85 'On just one February night . . .'. Beijing Daxue Lishixi, *Beijing shi*, p. 277.

p. 86 'Qing officials imprisoned the emissaries . . .'. See among other contemporary sources, Lieutenant-Colonel G. J. Wolseley, *Narrative of the War with China in 1860* (London, 1862), pp. 259–75.

p. 86 'After an orgy of looting . . .'. The 'inconvenient truths' of the participation of southern Chinese in the looting of the Yuanmingyuan, like the torture of the envoys, is generally not mentioned in ideologically driven Chinese histories of the events, but is attested to by such contemporary accounts as that of Comte Maurice d'Hérisson, quoted in Geremie Barmé, 'The Garden of Perfect Brightness, A Life in Ruins', *East Asian History*, XI (1996), pp. 134–5.

p. 93 'Geremie Barmé has written how the Boxers . . .'. Ibid., p. 139.

p. 99 'As a result of all these things . .'. For an account of the effect of the turmoil on the silk merchants and Chinese New Year's, see Chen Hu et al., *Beijing bainian wangshi: bu xunchangde shige 'zinian'* (*Ten Unusual Zi [Zodiac Cycle] Years in a Century of Beijing's History*) (Beijing, 2009), pp. 30–32.

p. 105 'The Yuanmingyuan yielded more stones and bricks . . .'. See Barmé, 'The Garden of Perfect Brightness', p. 140. All further details on the continued, post-1860 despoilment of the Yuanmingyuan come from Barmé's meticulous scholarship on this issue.

p. 105 'According to Strand . . .'. See David Strand, *Rickshaw Beijing: City People and Politics in the 1920s* (Berkeley, CA, 1989), pp. 205–6.

p. 105 'One out of four people in Beijing were poor . . .'. Madeleine Yue Dong, *Republican Beijing: The City and its Histories*

(Berkeley and Los Angeles, CA, 2003), Table 2: 'Distribution of Beijing Families by Economic Group, 1926', p. 215.

p. 105 'A Chinese researcher . . .'. Strand, *Rickshaw Beijing*, p. 42.

p. 109 'The wind found its way . . .'. Lao She, *Beneath the Red Banner*, trans. Don Cohn (Beijing, 1982), pp. 74–5.

p. 111 'A "rare and happy time for foreigners" . . .'. Fairbank made the observations quoted in this and the following paragraph in his review of Hugh Trevor-Roper's *Hermit of Peking: The Hidden Life of Sir Edmund Backhouse*, 'The Confidence Man', *New York Review of Books* (14 April 1977), www.nybooks.com.

p. 111 'Slipping into the luxurious calm . . .'. Susan Naquin, *Peking: Temples and City Life, 1400–1900* (Berkeley and Los Angeles, CA, and London, 2000), p. 699.

p. 112 'Even the monks of the Lama Temple . . .'. See Don Cohn and Zhang Jingqing, *Beijing Walks* (Hong Kong, 1993), pp. 203–7.

p. 113 'They imported huge quantities of drugs . . .'. Beijing Daxue Lishixi, *Beijing shi* (Beijing, 2003), p. 438.

p. 113 'Corruption blossomed and inflation bloomed . . .'. The price of flour comes from Chen Hu et al., *Beijing bainian wangshi*, p. 94.

p. 113 'In January 1949 . . .'. C. P. Fitzgerald is quoted in Geremie Barmé, *The Forbidden City* (London, 2008), p. 143.

pp. 114 'As the journalist-historian Dai Qing has observed . . .'. Dai Qing, 'How Peaceful was the Liberation of Beiping?', *China Heritage Quarterly*, XIV (2007), www.chinaheritagequarterly.org.

p. 114 'In May the Communist newspaper . . .'. These details come from Michael Meyer, *The Last Days of Old Beijing: Life in the Vanishing Backstreets of a City Transformed* (New York, 2008), p. 279.

pp. 114–15 'He'd written of Beijing . . .'. Liang Sicheng is quoted in Yue Dong, *Republican Beijing*, p. 29.

p. 115 'Liang raved to his friends . . .'. This detail comes from Xiao Hu, 'Preserving the Old Beijing: The First Conflict between Chinese Architects and the Communist Government in the 1950s', *James A. Rawley Graduate Conference in the Humanities*, Paper 8 (2006), p. 8, at http://digitalcommons.unl.edu.

p. 117 'His adopted daughter . . .'. Dai Qing, 'How Peaceful was the Liberation of Beiping?'.

p. 117 'Within one year of taking office . . .'. These figures are taken from Xiao Hu, 'Preserving the Old Beijing', p. 8.

p. 117 'Some were renamed to avoid confusion . . .'. See Cohn and Zhang Jingqing, *Beijing Walks*, p. 34.

p. 118 'The Palace Museum's first exhibition . . .'. See Barmé, *The Forbidden City*, p. 8.

p. 119 'The Communists' Soviet advisers . . .'. See Xiao Hu, 'Preserving the Old Beijing'.

p. 123 'Some 1,400 new factories . . .'. See Tiziano Terzani, *Behind the Forbidden Door* (London, 1986), p. 32.

p. 126 'In June 1959 an article appeared . . .'. Translated in Stephen G. Haw, *Beijing: A Concise History* (Oxford and New York, 2007), p. 119.

p. 126 'Though famine hit Beijing . . .'. Jasper Becker, *Hungry Ghosts: China's Secret Famine* (London, 1996), pp. 227–8.

p. 130 'One morning that August . . .'. See David Milton and Nancy Dall Milton, *The Wind Will Not Subside: Years in Revolutionary China, 1964–1969* (New York, 1976), p. 271.

p. 132 'In 1969 a shroud dropped . . .'. Details of this little-known and rarely discussed renovation can be found in Barmé, *The Forbidden City*, pp. 170–71.

p. 133 'China's carefully calibrated welcome . . .'. This account comes from Chen Hu et al., *Beijing bainian wangshi*, p. 134.

p. 133 'He toured the Forbidden City . . .'. See Barmé, *The Forbidden City*, p. 23.

pp. 133–4 'He rode the new No. 1 subway line . . .'. For more on Beijing's subway system at the time of Nixon's visit, see Sang Ye and Geremie Barmé, 'Beijing Underground: An Invisible City', *China Heritage Quarterly*, xiv (2008), www.chinaheritagequarterly.org. 'Neither subservient nor arrogant . . .'. For more on the reception given to Nixon, see Chen Hu et al., *Beijing bainian wangshi*, pp. 133–4.

p. 134 'Beijing's Xinhua Bookstore . . .'. These details are from Chen Hu et al., *Beijing bainian wangshi*, p. 138.

p. 135 'I weep while wolves and jackals laugh'. This famous line by Wang Lishan is translated by John Gittings in *China Changes Face* (Oxford and New York, 1989), p. 154.

p. 136 'Let me tell you, world . . .'. The translation of Bei Dao,

'The Answer', is by Bonnie S. McDougall and can be found in *Bulletin of Concerned Asian Scholars,* XVI/3 (1984), p. 27.

p. 140 'These entrepreneurial southerners . . .'. Xiang Biao has written the definitive history of Zhejiangcun. It has been translated by Jim Weldon and published as *Transcending Boundaries – Zhejiangcun: The Story of a Migrant Village in Beijing* (Leiden and Boston, 2005), pp. 1–2.

p. 142 'The Beijing Municipal Party Committee . . .'. Quoted and translated in Barmé and Minford, eds, *Seeds of Fire*, p. 400.

p. 146 'To the movement's sympathizers . . .'. The paradox of the 'tank man' is discussed in the opening sequence of the 1995 documentary *Gate of Heavenly Peace*, the transcript of which is available at The Gate of Heavenly Peace website, ww.tsquare.tv.

p. 148 Wang Shuo, *'Wanzhu', Xiexue juan, Wang Shuo Wenji ('The Operators', The Collected Writings of Wang Shuo, 'Satirical Works' Volume)* (Beijing, 1992), pp. 3–4.

p. 150 'According to Philip Pan . . .'. These details come from Richard Bernstein's review article 'The Death and Life of a Great Chinese City', *New York Review of Books* (26 March 2009), www.nybooks.com.

p. 151–3 'Between 1990 and 2007 . . .'. Statistics quoted in Meyer, *The Last Days of Old Beijing*, p. 293.

p. 154 'In 1954, having realized . . .'. See Xiao Hu, 'Preserving Old Beijing', p. 17.

p. 156 'Between 2001 and 2008 . . .'. This paragraph relies on veteran China correspondent Jaime FlorCruz's online report, 'China's Capital Still Getting Kick from 2008 Olympic Party', www.cnn.com, 2 July 2012. For the tourism angle, see Nelson Alcantara, 'Beijing: Post Olympics, Now and Beyond', www.eturbonews.com, 26 May 2010.

pp. 159–61 'In an article published in 2006 . . .'. An account of this fascinating incident can be found in 'On Stage and Screen', *China Heritage Quarterly*, VIII (2006), www.chinaheritagequarterly.org.

p. 162 'Linguists note . . .'. See Liu Yong et al., *Beijing lishi wenhua shiwu jiang*, p. 404.

p. 163 'Yet that year the photographer Xu Yong . . .'. See Jaime FlorCruz, 'China's Capital Still Getting Kick from 2008 Olympic Party', 2 July 2012, http://edition.cnn.com.

p. 168 Wang Jun, 'Qing liuxia Liang Sicheng, Lin Huiyin guju' ('Please Leave Be the Historic Home of Liang Shicheng and Lin Huiyin'), *City-Eye*, http://blog.sina.com.cn/wangjun, 10 July 2009.

p. 185 'The Nezha myth became entwined . . .'. David Der-wei Wang is quoted in Dong, *Republican Beijing*, p. 301.

p. 187 'In the twisting, teeming lanes . . .'. The descriptions of performers including 'Pockmark' Cao and the South City Amusement Park are drawn from the illustrated book on old Qianmen by Yang Xin, *Da Qianmen Wai* (*Outside Qianmen Gate*) (Beijing, 2003).

p. 188 'According to the writer Wang Jie . . .'. See Wang Jie, *Touguo jianzhu kan huangcheng guyun* (*Looking at the Imperial City through Architecture*) (Beijing, 2008), p. 140.

p. 190 'Given that the song was written in 1947 . . .'. See '*Alishande guniang*' ('Girl from Alishan'), www.baike.baidu.com.

p. 192 'As Pierre Ryckmans (Simon Leys) has observed . . .'. The essay was originally delivered as a Morrison Lecture at the Australian National University in 1986 and is republished in Simon Leys [Pierre Ryckmans], *Hall of Uselessness* (Melbourne, 2011), p. 252.

p. 198 'It was 1958 before the project got under way . . .'. All details of the secret history of Beijing's subway, including how it was tested with nuclear weapons, come from Sang Ye and Barmé, 'Beijing Underground: An Invisible City'.

p. 203 'So have the wells . . .'. See Andreas N. Angelakis et al., *Evolution of Water Supply through the Millennia* (London, 2012), p. 187.

p. 204–5 'Drought is not a new problem . . .'. Kangxi quoted and translated in Hok-Lam Chan, *Legends of the Building of Old Peking* (Hong Kong, 2008), p. 120.

p. 206 'There are controversial plans . . .'. See Tom Hancock, 'Water-starved Beijing Looks to the Sea', www.smartplanet.com, 27 October 2011.

p. 216 'It turned out that renting Segways . . .'. All references to Lawrence Liauw are from his 'Urbanization of Post-Olympic Beijing', in *Sustain and Develop: 306090 Books vol. 13*, ed. Joshua Bolchover and Jonathan D. Solomon (2010), at www.306090.com.

p. 219 'It was designed by Rem Koolhaas . . .'. All quotations from Martin Filler are from his article 'The Master of Bigness', *New York Review of Books* (10 May 2012), www.nybooks.com.

p. 220 'The *Asian Wall Street Journal* . . .'. Ron Gluckman's writing on Beijing architecture for the *Asian Wall Street Journal* and *Asiaweek* can be found at www.gluckman.com.

p. 232 'His trove included . . .'. See Liu Yong et al., *Beijing lishi wenhua shiwu jiang*, p. 56.

p. 235 'Their disciples included . . .'. Ibid., pp. 62–3.

p. 236 'As a result, as Geremie Barmé has written . . .'. This essay relies heavily on Geremie Barmé, 'Prince Gong's Folly', *China Heritage Quarterly*, XII (2007), www.chinaheritagequarterly.org.

Suggested Reading and Viewing

Books

Barmé, Geremie, *The Forbidden City* (London, 2008). The ultimate guide to the palace, its architecture and its history

Becker, Jasper, *City of Heavenly Tranquillity* (Oxford and New York, 2008). A veteran China journalist on the city, its history and its people

Bredon, Juliet, *Peking* (Shanghai, 1919). An elegant and informed portrait of the city and its places and customs written in the early twentieth century by a long-time resident

Chen Yongxiang and Hao Li, *Old Streets in Beijing* (Beijing, 2006). A bilingual, charmingly illustrated book about the old Beijing of commemorative arches, *hutong*, temples and courtyard homes

French, Paul, *Midnight in Peking* (Melbourne, 2011). The seamy side of foreign life on the eve of the Japanese invasion

Haw, Stephen G., *Beijing: A Concise History* (London, 2007). Just what the title promises: a concise history

Hok-Lam Chan, *Legends of the Building of Old Peking* (Hong Kong, 2008). Scholarly, somewhat esoteric, but fascinating: *the* source on Beijing's 'astral geography' and all things Nezha

Johnston, Reginald Fleming, *Twilight in the Forbidden City* (London, 1934). A first-person account by the tutor of the last emperor, Henry Puyi

Kates, George N., *The Years that were Fat: The Last of Old China* (Cambridge, MA, and London, 1952). An intelligent, sensitive and beautifully composed appreciation of Beijing in the 1930s

Lao She, *Camel Xiangzi*, trans. Shi Xiaoqing (Beijing, 1988). A classic novel of Beijing – as are all of Lao She's works, which so beautifully capture both the Beijing language and sensibility. Various editions abound (*Camel Xiangzi* is translated elsewhere as *Rickshaw Boy*)

Lin Haiyin, *My Memories of Old Beijing*, trans. Nancy Ing and Chi Pang-yuan (Hong Kong, 1992). A much-loved novel of *hutong* life in the first half of the twentieth century as seen through a young girl's eyes

Meyer, Michael, *The Last Days of Old Beijing: Life in the Vanishing Backstreets of a City Transformed* (New York, 2008; new edn with afterword, 2009). A personal, impeccably researched account of the destruction of the old 'Chinese City' south of Qianmen

Spence, Jonathan, *Emperor of China: Self-portrait of K'ang-Hi* (New York, 1975). A scholarly, imaginative recreation of the life of one of the greatest inhabitants of the Forbidden City by a leading historian of China

Films

Bertolucci, Bernardo, dir., *The Last Emperor* (1987). It's not perfect history but it is filmed in the Forbidden City and is full of atmosphere

Chen Kaige, dir., *Farewell My Concubine* (1993). A sweeping historical epic that follows the fate of two boys raised to be Peking Opera singers and evokes Beijing from the Republican era to Maoist times and beyond. Co-winner of the Palme d'Or at the Cannes International Film Festival in 1993

Gordon, Richard, and Carma Hinton, dirs, *Gate of Heavenly Peace* (1995). Award-winning documentary on the events of 1989

Jiang Wen, dir., *In the Heat of the Sun* (1994). A superb adaption of Wang Shuo's novel *Wild Beast*, about disaffected youth in Beijing in the final years of the Cultural Revolution

Wang Xiaoshuai, dir., *Beijing Bicycle* (2001). A migrant worker from the countryside goes in search of a stolen bicycle. Winner of the Jury Grand Prix at the Berlin International Film Festival in 2001

Online

For up-to-date listings on what's happening in Beijing, as well as where to eat, shop and find entertainment, see:

The Beijinger
www.thebeijinger.com

City Weekend Guide
www.cityweekend.com.cn/beijing

The Secret Guide to Alternative Beijing
www.alternativebeijing.com

That's Beijing
www.thatsmags.com/beijing

Time Out Beijing
www.timeoutbeijing.com

Acknowledgements

I am extremely grateful to Professor Geremie Barmé of the Australian National University and his Federation Fellowship project 'Beijing: China's Heritage and the City as Spectacle' for generous financial and practical support for this book. I thank the Australian National University School of Culture, History and Language in the ANU College of Asia and the Pacific for making me a Research Affiliate, and thus giving me access to the ANU's priceless library collections related to Beijing. RMIT University and the CAL (Creative Agency Ltd) Cultural Fund provided me with a month-long residency in Melbourne and access to university resources there. Geremie Barmé, Jeremy Goldkorn of Danwei.com, Kathy Bail, veteran Beijing correspondent Jane Macartney (a direct descendant of England's first emissary to Beijing, Lord Macartney) and Red Gate Gallery owner Brian Wallace all kindly read drafts or partial drafts of the manuscript and offered valuable suggestions and comments. Jeanne Moore graciously made available her extraordinary collection of old photographs and albums. Qin Taozi and Lois Conner, both of whom have devoted much of their brilliant careers to documenting this city, have been very generous in providing photographs. Dan Sanderson, Eveline Sun and Emma Johnston all contributed invaluably to the research, and Emma took a number of photographs for the book as well. Jade Muratore, Samantha Sperring and Naomi Jaivin (my mother), put in many hours typing corrections into the manuscript. Finally, I'd like to thank my tireless agent, Gaby Naher, and my patient, persistent and dedicated editors at Reaktion Books, Vivian Constantinopoulos and Aimee Selby.

Photo Acknowledgements

The author and publishers wish to express their thanks to the below sources of illustrative material and/or permission to reproduce it.

ahenobarbus: p. 223; © Trustees of the British Museum, London: p. 38; Lois Conner: pp. 10–11, 89, 123, 155, 157, 160, 162, 165; Corbis: pp. 16–17 (Gavin Hellier/JAI), 114 (Baldwin H. Ward & Kathryn C. Ward), 116, 137 (Bettmann), 144–5 (Peter Turnley); courtesy of Cui Jian: p. 142; das farbamt: p. 222; Charlie Fong: pp. 208, 218–19; Getty Images: p. 127; © Guan Wei: p. 149; image courtesy of the Historical Photographs of China © 2008 Penelope Fowler (http://hpc.vcea.net): p. 46; iStockphoto: pp. 60–61 (bjdlzx); Linda Jaivin: pp. 8–9, 18, 23, 24, 27, 28, 31, 33, 34, 37, 40, 50–51, 52, 62, 82, 85, 87, 108–9, 141, 172, 174, 175, 177, 182, 184, 190, 191, 194, 201, 214, 215, 217, 229, 230; Emma Johnston: pp. 13, 67, 232, 233, 234, 235, 238; Michael Leaman: pp. 227, 237; Library of Congress, Washington, DC: pp. 74–5 , 79, 90–91, 94, 95, 96, 99, 107, 120; National Archives, Washington, DC: p. 133; Qin Taozi: pp. 6–7, 147, 152, 163, 168–9, 213; Ran and Hat600: p. 198; Rex Features: pp. 128 (courtesy Everett Collection), 140 (Grace/Keystone USA); Dan Sanderson: pp. 70–71, 124–5, 167, 205; Shizhao: pp. 49, 77; Shutterstock: pp. 12 (testing), 59 (Max Studio), 135 (Mario Savola), 180 (Nadby Aizat); Victoria & Albert Museum, London: p. 84; Wang Jinlang (dir.), *Beijing Besieged by Waste*, image courtesy of the dGenerate Collection at Icarus Films, www.icarusfilms.com: p. 164; WiNG: p. 221; © Xu Bing Studio: pp. 14–15; Zhangzhe0101: pp. 44–5

Index

Page numbers in italics refer to illustrations